V

19

 Sefton Libraries Bookface   @seftonLibraries   Sefton Libraries

Your library Sefton

Please return this item by the due date:

Please return this item by the due date
or renew at **www.sefton.gov.uk/libraries**
or by telephone at **any** Sefton library:

Bootle Library   **0151 934 5781**
Crosby Library   **0151 257 6400**
Formby Library   **01704 874 177**
Meadows Library   **0151 288 6727**
Netherton Library   **0151 525 0607**
Southport Library   **0151 934 2118**

your Library Sefton

Sefton Council

Also covers Microsoft Word in Office 365

In easy steps is an imprint of In Easy Steps Limited
16 Hamilton Terrace · Holly Walk · Leamington Spa
Warwickshire · United Kingdom · CV32 4LY

www.ineasysteps.com

Notice of Liability
Every effort has been made to ensure that this book contains accurate
and current information. However, In Easy Steps Limited and the
author shall not be liable for any loss or damage suffered by readers
as a result of any information contained herein.

Trademarks
Microsoft®, Office 365® and Windows® are registered trademarks
of Microsoft Corporation. All other trademarks are acknowledged as
belonging to their respective companies.

In Easy Steps Limited supports The Forest Stewardship Council (FSC),
the leading international forest certification organization. All our titles
that are printed on Greenpeace approved FSC certified paper carry the
FSC logo.

MIX
Paper from
responsible sources
FSC® C020837
www.fsc.org

Printed and bound in the United Kingdom

ISBN 978-1-84078-822-8

Contents

1 Finding your way around

This chapter quickly gets you started with Word 2019. It shows you how to launch Word and explains all the main areas in its screen layout. You'll try some basic text editing as well as the main controls and how they are organized and accessed.

It's very important to experiment using your own examples – trying techniques a few times on test documents will give you the confidence you'll need when working for real.

If you need guidance on using the Windows operating environment, check out our Windows 10 titles: **Windows 10 in easy steps** and **Windows 10 for Seniors in easy steps**.

The New icon pictured above indicates a new or enhanced feature introduced with the latest version of Word.

Introduction

Word processing was one of the first popular applications for the modern personal computer. In the early days it provided little more than the ability to enter and change text on the screen. Today, many more people have computers and tablets at home and in the office, and virtually all use a word processor regularly. As the years have passed, the capabilities of the computer and its software have dramatically increased, far beyond the expectations of the early generations of users back in the 1970s and '80s.

Almost since the beginning, Microsoft Word has been acknowledged as a leader in its field. It is one of the best selling software applications in any category. It grew in complexity from a program with a handful of menu commands to one with an astonishing array of features.

In creating Word 2019, Microsoft has built logically on the foundation of the previous versions. Rather than relying on complex menus, Word works with tabbed visual controls that reconfigure themselves to suit what you're currently doing. Accordingly, this book works as a graphical teaching guide – wherever possible, pictures and worked examples are used to demonstrate concepts. It's not intended to replace Microsoft's documentation; instead you should view it as a way of getting up to speed quickly in a wide range of useful techniques.

The full range of Word's features is covered in this and the following chapters – from creating and editing simple text-based documents to tables, graphics and research tools as well as more advanced techniques such as viewing and editing documents on the web.

How to use this book

To gain maximum benefit from this book, make sure you're first familiar with the Windows operating environment (using the mouse, icons, menus, dialog boxes and so on). There are a number of books in the **In Easy Steps** range that can help you here.

It's a good idea to start off by going through Chapters 1 and 2 fairly thoroughly, since these introduce basic concepts that are added to later on. Once you've done this, feel free to dip into the other chapters as you like.

Starting Word 2019

The way in which you start Word depends on whether you're using a desktop PC or a tablet, and the operating system version.

From Windows 10

1 Click the Windows Start button and look through the list

2 If Word isn't in the "Recently added" or "Most used" sections, scroll through the alphabetical list and choose Word

3 Alternatively, type "Word" into the text box "Type here to search" next to the Windows Start button

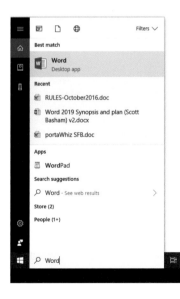

4 You will see a list of matches in various categories including Recent, Apps and Store

5 Click on "Word" in the list of matching applications

Hot tip

In earlier versions of Windows you can search in a similar way via the Charms bar. Press WinKey + C then click the Search icon. If you are using a tablet or touchscreen, swipe inwards from the right edge of the screen.

Installing Word in the taskbar

If you use Word regularly then it might be a good idea to have a quick way of launching from the Desktop.

For more details and help on accessing and organizing applications and documents, check the range of books in the **In Easy Steps** series. There are a number of books covering each version of the Windows operating system.

1 From the Start button, or via the Search option, locate Word

2 Select by right-clicking to see a pop-up menu

3 Click the button "Pin to taskbar" (click More first if necessary)

4 You can now launch Word directly from the taskbar. To remove it, right-click on the icon and choose "Unpin from taskbar"

Opening a document directly from Windows Explorer

On most PCs, Word document files will be recognized and shown with a distinctive icon as shown below.

1 Locate your Word document using Search or the Windows File Explorer

2 Clicking on a search result or double-clicking in File Explorer will launch the associated program (in this case, Word) and automatically open the file

DP Project Closure Report new theme.docx

DP Project Closure Report3.docx

SFB Report1.docx

If you right-click on an application in the Start Menu and choose More > "Open file location" you will go to a folder containing the shortcut icons for Word and other Office applications. If you don't want Word on the taskbar, then consider copying the shortcut(s) to the Desktop for quick access.

The initial screen

If you launched Word directly (not via a document) then you will see the following screen.

This initial screen also lets you start a new document using one of the installed templates. These are special documents with distinctive designs, where you can easily substitute in your own content. It is possible to download additional templates, or even to create your own.

1 For a simple blank page, click "Blank document"

2 If you already have a document to view or edit, check to see if it's in the Recent list on the left side of the screen

3 If your document is there, click to open it. If not, click the Open Other Documents link in the lower left corner. The Browse button takes you to the Open dialog box

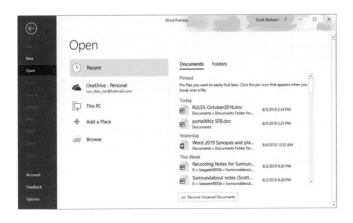

The main screen

Once Word is up and running, you should see the following screen – with all the elements illustrated here:

Quick Access Toolbar

Command tabs

Document title

Mini Toolbar

Status bar   Main page   View icons   Zoom

Don't forget

Don't worry if your screen doesn't exactly match this illustration: Word's display is highly customizable and most visual elements can be switched on or off according to your own preferences. You will find tips on how to do this throughout the book.

You can resize Word's window in the normal way by dragging on its border (if it's maximized then you'll need to click the Restore Down button ⬜ first).

As you can see from the two illustrations on this page, Word automatically resizes and reconfigures its workspace and controls to make the best use of the space available.

If you can't see the icon or control you want, simply make the window larger or click the ▾ symbol to see what's been hidden.

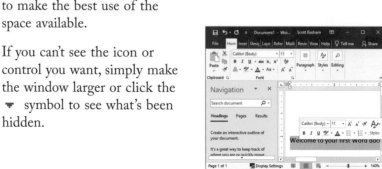

The Ribbon

Near the top of the screen is the Ribbon, which gives you access to most of Word's controls within a few mouse clicks. It's divided into a number of tabs, only one of which is active at any time. In the example below, the Home tab is showing basic text editing and formatting features.

In this example the highlighted text changes its appearance as the controls in the Ribbon are used. It is currently formatted using the style "Normal". If the mouse hovers over the style "Heading 1", the text temporarily changes its format to preview this style. For more about text styles see Chapter 2.

Using different tabs in the Ribbon

1 Click on the Insert tab's title to activate it. You'll see it's subdivided into 10 sections

2 Each section contains groups of related controls. Let your mouse hover over one of these to see a brief explanation

...cont'd

Hot tip

If you click on the Ribbon Display Options ![icon] icon at the top right of the screen you can change how the Ribbon and tabs will display.

③ Double-click on the currently-active tab to hide the ribbon temporarily. This is useful if you want to maximize the amount of screen space available for viewing and editing your document

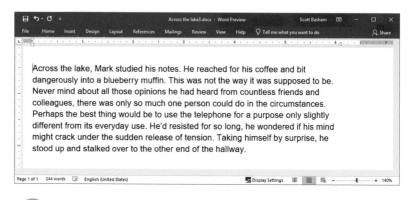

④ When the Ribbon is hidden in this way, clicking on a tab heading will temporarily reveal its contents. Double-click on a tab to restore the Ribbon permanently

⑤ Click on the File tab to see document information, together with other options for managing documents including printing, sharing and exporting. There is also a range of global options and account tools

Don't forget

Word integrates seamlessly with a range of connected services such as OneDrive and YouTube, provided you are logged in to a valid Microsoft online account. See Chapter 8 "Sharing features" for more on this topic.

The Mini Toolbar

Whenever you have some text selected, the Mini Toolbar will appear nearby. It gives you immediate access to the most commonly-used text formatting options.

Font   Size   Larger   Smaller   Format painter

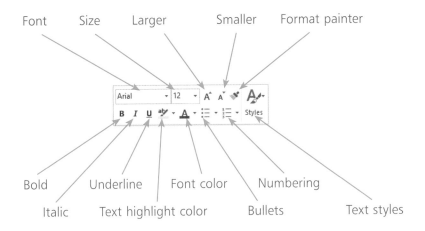

Bold   Underline   Font color   Numbering

Italic   Text highlight color   Bullets   Text styles

Using the Mini Toolbar

1 Type some text and then select it by clicking and dragging across it with the mouse

2 The Mini Toolbar will appear automatically just above the text, as in the illustration below

3 Click on one of the controls within the Mini Toolbar to change the appearance of your selected text

4 Repeat the process with other selected areas of text

Some of the Mini Toolbar's controls have keyboard shortcuts. For example, bold can be set On and Off by typing Ctrl + B, and italic with Ctrl + I. To find out if a control has a shortcut, simply hover over it with the mouse pointer for a few moments. There is a handy reference table of keyboard shortcuts in the inside front cover of this book.

If the Mini Toolbar fails to appear when you hover over selected text with your mouse, try right-clicking. A pop-up context menu will appear with the Mini Toolbar immediately above.

The Quick Access Toolbar

The Quick Access Toolbar is the small collection of tools at the top of the screen above the File tab.

Save   Undo   Repeat   Customize

Touch/Mouse Mode lets you choose between the best control layout for mouse or touch input. Touch input adds more space between commands and controls; this makes it easier to operate Word with a touchscreen.

Customizing the Quick Access Toolbar

1   Click the Customize icon on the Quick Access Toolbar and select a command or choose More Commands to see the full list. Note there is also an option to place the Toolbar below the Ribbon

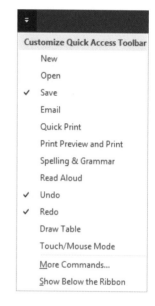

2   In the dialog, select from the Choose commands from drop-down list to see a list of Word commands

3   If you want customizations to be global, make sure "For all documents" is selected in the top right corner

If you use the Quick Access Toolbar's Undo button then a Redo button becomes available. Undo and Redo together allow you to step backwards and forwards through your actions.

...cont'd

4 Add icons by double-clicking in the left-hand list, or click once to select and then choose Add>>

In this illustration you can see that Quick Access Toolbar is the highlighted item at the left of the dialog. If you select the Customize Ribbon option directly above then you will have the opportunity to completely redesign Word's layout of controls.

5 Remove icons by double-clicking in the right-hand list, or click once to select and then choose <<Remove

6 You can control the order in which the icons appear in the Toolbar. To do this, select a command in the right-hand list then use the Up arrow and Down arrow buttons to change its position. The top item in the list will appear as the first icon at the left of the Toolbar

In this illustration we selected the Read Aloud tool – this is a new feature illustrated in Chapter 10 "Tools for reviewing".

7 Click OK when done, or Cancel to abandon your changes. The Quick Access Toolbar will now show the icons you've selected

From the Customize Quick Access Toolbar dialog you can reset the Toolbar to its initial state by clicking the Reset button. It's also possible to import and export your customizations to a file.

You can also access these settings by activating the File tab, choosing Options, then selecting Quick Access Toolbar.

17

The Status bar

This bar at the bottom of the screen shows settings and options.

Customizing the Status bar

1 Right-click anywhere on the Status bar to see options

2 A tick beside an item means it's displayed in the Status bar. Click to toggle On and Off

The Status bar also shows you current page, number of words, spelling/grammar information and zoom-level controls.

In this illustration we can see that the Vertical Page Position is 2.7 inches.

Tell Me

1 Type some text in the area "Tell me what you want to do"

2 Word will show you related commands, or options for searching Word help or using Smart Lookup

Smart Lookup makes use of a combination of sources including dictionaries, Wikipedia and more general web searches.

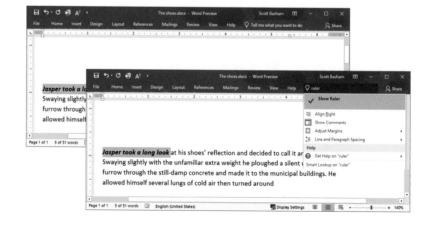

Getting help

1 Move your mouse over a command in the Ribbon. After a few moments a tooltip appears, showing you the name of the command (this is useful if it's displayed only as an icon in the Ribbon). You'll also see an explanation of its function

2 The icon indicates that a dialog box will open if you click on it. If you hover over it you'll see a preview of that dialog

3 For more information about Word's features, press an ⓘ icon (if available) and a pop-up window will appear

Help is available in most of Word's dialogs and screens.

4 For more detail, click on the question mark icon in the top right-hand corner of a dialog box or press the F1 key. If your mouse was not pointing at any controls when you pressed F1 then a general searchable Help window appears

Text editing

Text editing in Word is no different to programs such as Notepad, WordPad, Outlook, or PowerPoint. If you're already familiar with these basic skills then you can skip ahead to the next section.

Getting started

1 Start up Word so that you have a new blank document. If Word is already open then click on the File tab, then choose New, then "Blank document"

2 Enter some example text; enough for a line or two. Don't worry if you make mistakes as these will be easy to correct later on. Look for the flashing vertical line, known as the insertion point, which indicates where any new text will appear

Don't forget

The words to the right of the insertion point will automatically move along to accommodate any text you are inserting.

Things should be explained as simply as possible, but no simpler

3 You can easily move the insertion point anywhere in your text by clicking with the mouse. The arrow keys will also let you move up, down, left and right within any existing text. Move your insertion point so that it's somewhere in the middle of your text

4 If you type more text now it will be inserted at your current position. To remove text, use the Backspace key to delete the character to the left of your current position, or the Delete key to remove the character to the right. If you hold down either of these keys for more than a moment they will "repeat" and start deleting more characters

Hot tip

Word automatically works out when to start a new line without breaking words. If you want to force a new line, for example to begin a new paragraph, press the Return key or the Enter key.

Selecting text

Basic techniques

Selecting text is almost always the first step when formatting or editing, so it's worth knowing all the different techniques. There are quite a few methods for text selection that work consistently across many applications on your PC or Mac such as double-clicking to select a word. As you'd expect, this works in Word so now we'll look at this plus some more options.

1 Click and drag over the text you want to select. This is quick and easy for small amounts of text

2 If the wrong text is highlighted, click anywhere in the text editing area to cancel the selection, then try again

3 Double-click on a word to select it. Triple-click to select a paragraph. If you're using a touchscreen, tap twice to begin selecting then drag the circular handles to adjust the start and end of the selection

Using the arrow keys, or a mouse click, or a tap on a touchscreen, allows you to reposition your insertion point anywhere within the text. If you try to move beyond the existing text you'll find that the insertion point refuses to move. One way around this is to move just to the right of the last character and then add more text.

Don't be tempted to add extra spacing by pressing the spacebar many times. Although this will work up to a point, it's not the most flexible way of controlling spacing. You'll learn much better techniques for this in the next two chapters.

...cont'd

More advanced techniques

It's worth experimenting with selection techniques, as after a while you'll be able to choose the best method each time instinctively.

1 Move your mouse into the left margin area. You can tell that you are in the correct area if the cursor turns into an arrow pointing to the right instead of to the left

2 Drag vertically to select whole lines of text

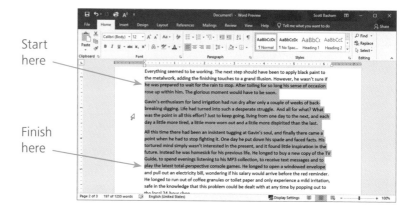

Start here

Finish here

3 The easiest way to select larger amounts very precisely is to click the mouse at the start of the text

4 Locate the end of the area, scrolling if necessary

5 Hold down the Shift key and click. All text between the start and end will be selected. If you accidentally clicked at the wrong endpoint, simply Shift + click again

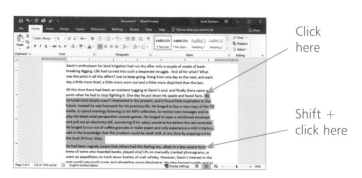

Click here

Shift + click here

Hot tip

You can quickly select all the text in your document by clicking on the Select option in the editing section of the Home tab, and choosing Select All. The keyboard shortcut for this is Ctrl + A.

Hot tip

If you hold down the Shift key when clicking in the left margin area, the current selection will be extended up to the point where you clicked.

Discontinuous text selection

1 Select some text using any of the previous techniques

2 Now, holding down the Control key, click and drag across some text that is separate from your original selection

3 Repeat this process to add more areas to your selection

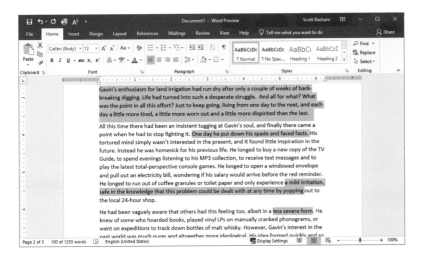

Anything you type, even a single character, will normally replace all selected text. For example, if you have three paragraphs selected and you accidentally press the spacebar, then all that text will be replaced with the space. If this happens, simply use the Undo button in the Quick Access Toolbar, or type Ctrl + Z.

23

Selection with the Alt key

If you click and drag while holding the Alt key down, you'll select all text in a rectangular area. This is fun, although of questionable practical use.

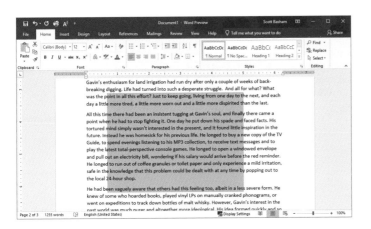

Working with files

Chapter 7 "Files and settings" will look at file manipulation in detail, so for now we'll just concentrate on the simplest way to store and retrieve your work.

Starting a new document

 When you start up Word you'll automatically be shown options for beginning a new document. If you're already using Word and are ready to create another new document, select the File tab and click New

Saving your work

 If you attempt to close down Word without saving you'll see the following message. Click Save if you want to save your work before quitting

Hot tip

If you accidentally shut down Word you might still have a chance to recover your work. When you reopen the document a message may appear, giving you the option of using the most up-to-date version of your document. In some cases this may be a copy Word saved automatically for you.

...cont'd

2 Another way to save your work is to click on the Save icon in the Quick Access Toolbar. If you have saved the document previously, Word simply saves using the same name and file location as before. If this is the first time for saving the document, you'll see the following screen

Hot tip

If your document has already been saved, but you want to save a new copy rather than overwrite the previous version, go to the File tab and select Save As instead of Save.

3 Click on one of the places listed then choose a folder by clicking (or use the Browse button), then click Save in the next dialog

Opening a saved document

1 Select the File tab then click Open

Don't forget

If you haven't yet started up Word then you can speed things up by locating your document then double-clicking on its icon. This will start up Word and open the document automatically.

2 Under Open, choose Recent, the online storage options, This PC, or Browse to access a local file

3 If you chose Browse then click through the structure of folders and select a file in the standard Windows dialog

Click and type

Provided you are in Word's Print Layout or Web Layout view, you can easily add text anywhere on the page.

1 First make sure that Print Layout view is selected from the Page View icons in the Status bar at the bottom of the screen

Print Layout view

Don't forget

If click and type doesn't appear to work, click on the File tab and choose Options. Select Advanced and make sure that the option "Enable click and type" is activated.

2 Move over a blank area. The pointer icon will indicate to you whether new text will be aligned left, right or centered. The example below shows the icon for centered text. Double-click to establish a new insertion point

Give me a lever long enough and a fulcrum on which to place it, and I shall move the world.

3 Type in some new text. Word will create any new blank lines necessary to allow the text to be positioned correctly. It also applies the correct form of alignment

Hot tip

You'll learn more about controlling left, right and centered text in Chapter 2.

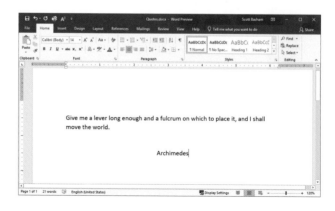

Give me a lever long enough and a fulcrum on which to place it, and I shall move the world.

Archimedes

Basic navigation

When your text is too large for the document window, you'll need to use one of the following navigation methods:

Scroll up

Scroll box

Scroll down

Scroll left   Scroll box   Scroll right

The scroll boxes' positions let you know where you are in a document. For example, when the vertical scroll box is at the top of the scroll bar, you are looking at the top (the beginning) of the document.

Quick ways to scroll

1 Drag the scroll box directly to a new position

2 Click in the scroll bar to either side of the scroll box. The document will immediately scroll in that direction one screen at a time

3 As you move your insertion point with the arrow keys on the keyboard, Word will scroll so that it can always be seen

4 If your mouse has a wheel, this can usually be used to scroll vertically through your document

5 The PgUp (Page Up) and PgDn (Page Down) keys will move you up and down one screen at a time

6 If you have a touch-enabled screen, place your finger inside the text area and swipe up or down to scroll

As you scroll down, the scroll box moves like an elevator down a shaft. The size of the box indicates how much of the document you can see (if the box occupies a third of the scroll bar, then you're viewing a third of the document).

...cont'd

Zooming

This allows you to control the level of magnification on screen. The zoom controls are in the bottom-right corner.

Remember to consider the size of Word's main window – in most cases it should be maximized. Note, however, that in this book we often use smaller windows so that we can concentrate on a particular part of the screen or set of controls.

Zoom out   Adjust zoom level   Zoom in   Zoom level

The Zoom dialog box

1 Click on the "Zoom level" icon (displayed as "55%" in the example above) to open the Zoom dialog box

2 Choose one of the options, or enter a percentage value directly. "Text width" is a good option to use if you like to avoid horizontal scrolling

3 Click OK to apply the zoom level

Themes for Word's interface

There are two types of Themes in Word. In Chapter 4 "Structured documents" we'll see how Themes in the Design tab can give you a powerful set of controls to quickly change the overall design of your document. The other type of Theme, accessible from the Options dialog, lets you change the overall user interface for Word.

Changing the Theme

1 Go to the File tab and choose Options

2 The General section of the dialog appears by default. Under "Personalize your copy of Microsoft Office" select a different Office Theme

The Black Theme is a new addition introduced with Word 2019.

3 When you click OK you will see Word's interface and general color scheme for windows, controls and dialogs change. This does not affect your documents' contents

Word 2019 vs Office 365

Word 2019 and Office 365 are closely related. Most of the features and techniques you'll see explained in this book will work equally well with both versions. So what exactly is the difference between them?

Office 365 has for some time been Microsoft's Cloud-based subscription service, giving businesses and individuals access to the entire range of Office products. Cloud-based services provide easy synchronization of files and remote access. Another key difference is how the user pays for the software. For a subscription service, such as Office 365, payments are made monthly or yearly. The user is effectively renting rather than buying software outright. This means a smaller initial outlay, but the cost is ongoing.

Word 2019 as a product comes with a perpetual license, so this is a one-off purchase. Microsoft recognizes that some people prefer this concept of ownership, and also that some are not yet interested in the features and benefits of Cloud-based services.

If you go to the File tab and choose Account you'll see which version of Word you're using. You can also control how often updates are downloaded and installed.

There is another important difference when it comes to support and updates for Word. If you're using Office 365 then its software is in support as long as you keep paying the subscription. Furthermore, when Microsoft is ready to add new features to the Office applications then these updates are automatically installed and available to the user.

Word 2019, on the other hand, has its feature set frozen at the time it's released. Microsoft will offer support for security and bug fixes over a set period of years – certainly for some time after the next version of Word is released. However, new features are not added continuously as with Office 365. To get extra functionality you'll either need to purchase a newer version of Word (when it's released) or switch to an Office 365 subscription.

2 Basic editing

Now that you know your way around, we'll look at the most common techniques for text editing and formatting.

The Clipboard

The Clipboard is a temporary storage area that can hold text or even other items such as graphic images. It can be used to help you move or copy text you have selected. It's also usually possible to use it to transfer text between different applications.

Cut and paste

1 Select the text to be moved. Choose Cut from the Clipboard section at the left of the Home tab

Hot tip

You can also use Ctrl + X to cut text, or right-click on your selection and choose Cut from the pop-up menu.

2 The text is removed and put onto the Clipboard. Now, place your insertion point at the desired destination and right-click. A pop-up menu appears offering you a choice of four paste options

Keep Source Formatting   Merge Formatting   Paste as Picture   Keep Text Only

NEW

Paste as Picture is a new addition introduced with Word 2019. You'll learn more about Pictures in Chapter 5.

3 The source text was 18 point Calibri bold. If you want to use these attributes, click on the Keep Source Formatting option. If you want to use the attributes already at the destination, click on Keep Text Only. In the following example we right-clicked in an area of 12 point Times New Roman normal text and chose Keep Text Only

...cont'd

Even after you've pasted text you can still change your mind about the paste formatting options.

Altering paste options after pasting

1 After you've pasted text you'll see the Paste Options icon nearby. Either click the icon or press the Ctrl key to review the available paste options

2 In the example below we chose the second option: Merge Formatting. The font and size are that of the destination, but the bold effect has been taken from the source

3 The Paste Options are available to you until you start typing, at which point the icon disappears

4 If you change your mind after this, then repeatedly click Undo until you've gone back to the point just before pasting, then paste once again. The Paste Options icon should appear once more

The Clipboard tools give you instant access to Cut, Copy and Paste in the form of icons:

33

You can cut and paste using the keyboard shortcuts Ctrl + X and Ctrl + V respectively.

...cont'd

Copy and paste

1 Select the text you want to copy, right-click and choose Copy from the pop-up menu

You can also click on the Copy and Paste icons in the Clipboard tools. A third way to copy and paste is to use the keyboard shortcuts Ctrl + C and Ctrl + V respectively.

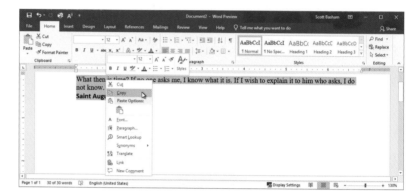

2 Place the insertion point at the destination for the copied text, right-click and choose the appropriate paste option

3 Pasting text doesn't actually remove it from the Clipboard, so you can paste the same text many times

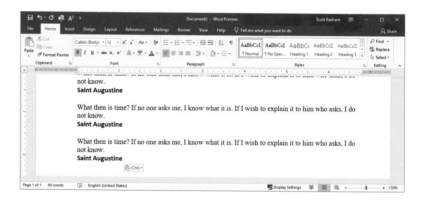

4 If you select some text before pasting, then the pasted text usually replaces what's selected. This feature can be switched on and off from File > Options > Advanced (at the top of the dialog box is an option: "Typing replaces selected text")

The Spike

The Spike is similar to the Clipboard in that it's a temporary storage area for text. The main difference is that you can add more and more text onto the Spike with a keyboard shortcut.

1 Select some text and type Ctrl + F3. The text disappears. It has been impaled on the Spike

35

Hot tip

You can repeat this more times if you want to collect more pieces of text onto the Spike. Each time you press Ctrl + F3, any selected text is removed from the page and added to the Spike. Note, however, that you only press Ctrl + Shift + F3 once – as soon as the text is back on the page it has been removed from the Spike.

2 Move to a second piece of text and repeat the process: select then type Ctrl + F3

3 Repeat until you have collected all your text. Then move your insertion point to your target location and type Ctrl + Shift + F3 to paste it back into your document

The Format Painter

This is an easy way to copy attributes from one place to another.

1 Select a sample of text that has the desired attributes

2 Click the Format Painter icon in the Clipboard section of the Home tab. This "loads" the icon with the attributes of the selected text

To copy formatting from the current selection to more than one destination, simply double-click on the Format Painter icon. You can then apply the formatting to as many pieces of text as you wish. When you've finished, either click back on the icon to discharge the loaded attributes or press the Escape key.

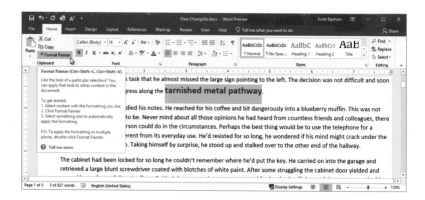

3 The pointer has changed its appearance to indicate that there are attributes loaded. Drag across your target to apply these settings

This is a very powerful feature so remember you can always click Undo if the results are not what you wanted.

This normally just copies character-level attributes. However, if you select an entire paragraph, click the Format Painter, then select an entire destination paragraph, all attributes (including paragraph settings such as alignment) will be copied.

Formatting characters

The Home tab contains the controls you'll use most often, so it's selected by default whenever you open or create a document.

It's organized into five areas: Clipboard, Font, Paragraph, Styles and Editing controls. We'll start by looking at the Font controls.

Choosing the font with the Mini Toolbar

The terms "font" and "typeface" come from traditional typography, and describe the visual design of letters and other symbols. Most people will be familiar with popular typefaces such as Arial or Times New Roman. Strictly speaking, a font is an instance of a typeface at a certain size and variant such as normal, light, bold or italic. These days the term "font" is often used in place of typeface, so in Word we might select a font of "Arial Black", then choose a size of 12 and perhaps apply an effect such as italic.

Hot tip

Font size is usually measured in points, where 72 points is equal to one inch when printed. Most printed body text is either 10, 11 or 12 points in size.

37

1 Select the text you wish to format. If you keep your mouse near the selected area, the Mini Toolbar will be visible

2 Select from the font menu in the Mini Toolbar. The list is previewed using the fonts themselves. Recently-used fonts are listed near the top

Don't forget

If the Mini Toolbar fails to appear when you hover over some text with your mouse, try right-clicking. A pop-up context menu will appear with the Mini Toolbar immediately above.

The keyboard shortcuts for Bold, Italic and Underline are Ctrl + B, Ctrl + I and Ctrl + U respectively.

Formatting with the Home tab

The Font section of the Home tab gives you access to more ways of controlling the appearance of characters.

1 Select some text. Change font, size, and other attributes by selecting from the Font section in the Home tab

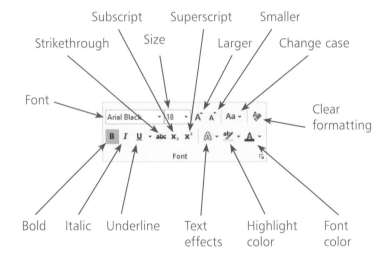

2 The Font area shows the current settings of selected text, wherever possible

3 In this example all the selected text is 18 point in size, and bold, so that's shown in the Font area. However, since the text uses more than one font, the area that usually displays the font name is blank. Selecting just the word "Phaedrus", or even part of that word, would cause the Font area to show "Arial Black"

...cont'd

The Font dialog

You can call up the Font dialog box to get full character-level control over the appearance of your selected text.

1 Select some text. Click on the dialog icon in the lower-right corner of the Font area, or press Ctrl + D

Open Font dialog

2 You now have access to additional effects, such as double strikethrough, and a variety of underline styles. The Preview box near the bottom gives you an indication of how the text would appear if you clicked OK

Font ? ✕

Fo̲nt **Ad̲vanced**

F̲ont:	Font st̲yle:	Si̲ze:
Arial Black	Bold	18
Adobe Song Std L ⌃ Aerospace BT Aldine401 BT Arial Arial Black ⌄	Regular ⌃ Italic Bold Bold Italic ⌄	11 ⌃ 12 14 16 18 ⌄

Font c̲olor:	U̲nderline style:	Underline color:
Automatic ⌄	(none) ⌄	Automatic ⌄

Effects

☐ Stri̲kethrough   ☐ S̲mall caps
☐ Doub̲le strikethrough   ☐ A̲ll caps
☐ Su̲perscript   ☐ H̲idden
☐ Su̲bscript

Preview

```
              Phaedrus
```

This font style is imitated for display. The closest matching style will be printed.

Set As D̲efault   Text E̲ffects...   OK   Cancel

Hot tip

Clicking the Text Effects button will take you to a dialog where you can apply a wide range of visual effects to your text. These include fills, outlines, shadow, reflections and 3D formats. You can apply some (but not all) of these directly from icons in the Home tab of the Ribbon, as you will see in the example on page 41.

...cont'd

Click on the Advanced tab to control the precise positioning and scaling of the selected characters

Scaling allows you to stretch or compress text horizontally. While this can sometimes work well for large titles, it's not recommended for use on main text as the results are often unreadable. If you need narrower or wider text then try using a different font that is already the desired shape.

Kerning

Kerning is a process used to adjust the space between certain combinations of characters. For example, when the letters "T" and "o" occur next to each other, normal spacing appears too wide. If you activate kerning then they will be brought closer together to create the illusion of normal spacing. Since kerning creates more work for your computer when drawing text on the screen it may increase the time it takes to display. For this reason, you might want to activate it only for larger font sizes (where spacing is more noticeable).

Ligatures

The Advanced dialog also has the ability to access a range of OpenType features. OpenType allows font designers to make use of features such as special small caps, ligatures, number forms and spacing. Ligatures are combinations of characters designed as a single entity. In this example you can see that applying ligatures affects the two consecutive "f" characters, which are displayed as a specially designed single character.

To   To

Unkerned   Kerned

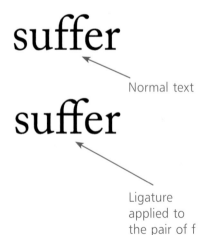

suffer

Normal text

suffer

Ligature applied to the pair of f characters

You might not notice any changes in the appearance of your text when you activate ligatures, as this setting will only make a difference if you are using a font that has been specially created with ligature information.

Text effects

Word gives you access to a wide range of text effects, and by using the Font area of the Home tab you'll get an instant preview.

1 Select some text. Click on the "Text Effects and Typography" button within the Font tools to see a menu of popular effects. As you hover over an item your text will temporarily preview the effect. Either move to a different effect or, if you are happy with your selection, click once on the effect to apply it permanently

The Text Highlight Color and the Font Color buttons also give you an instant preview of how the text will look as you hover over each color in their pop-up menus.

2 You can use the sub-menus to access more options within the individual effects of outline, shadow, reflection, and glow. Note that you can apply several effects at once, although just one from each category. For example, an outer shadow, a green glow and a medium reflection can all be applied to a single piece of text, as in the following example

Formatting paragraphs

The Mini Toolbar gives you the ability to switch centering On and Off, adjust the left indent or create a bulleted list. For most paragraph-level attributes, however, you'll use the Paragraph section of the Home tab.

Alignment

1 If you want to change just one paragraph then simply click anywhere within it. To change multiple paragraphs, select them using any of the techniques seen earlier

2 Click on one of the alignment icons to choose left, centered, right, or justified alignment. There is an example of each type illustrated below

Justified text has a straight edge at both the left and the right margins (apart from the final line in a paragraph). This is done by adjusting the spacing between words.

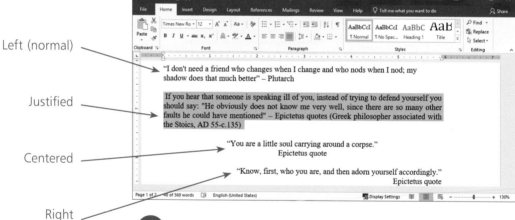

Left (normal)

Justified

Centered

Right

3 To see more paragraph controls, click the small open dialog icon ▪ in the lower-right corner of this section. The dialog that appears has two tabbed pages: "Indents and Spacing" and "Line and Page Breaks". These give you accurate control over attributes such as line spacing, indentation, and hyphenation

4 Click OK in the dialog to view the changes to the text, or Cancel to discard any changes you made while in the dialog

Remember that a heading is regarded by Word as a single-line paragraph.

Bulleted lists

1 Enter the text for your list, pressing the Return key after each item. Select this text

2 Open the Bullets pop-up menu in the Paragraph area of the Home tab

Hot tip

A quick way to create a bulleted list is to type an asterisk at the beginning of the first line. Word will automatically change this to a bullet, and format this and all subsequent lines for you. When you have finished, leave the next line blank and just press Return. Word will then switch off the bulleted effect.

3 Choose the bullet type. If you don't like any of those displayed then choose Define New Bullet. From this dialog you can select any symbol or picture

Hot tip

From the Define New Bullet dialog you can choose any image or character from a font for your bullet. Many fonts, such as Wingdings and Dingbats, are pictorial – this makes them a good source for bullets.

...cont'd

Numbered lists

If you choose Control AutoFormat Options you will call up a dialog with settings for this plus many other automatic features.

1 If you enter a new line of text beginning with a "1." then Word will automatically start to create a numbered list for you. When you press Return the next numbered line will be created for you automatically, and so on until you press Return twice to indicate the end of the list

2 This behavior may not always be what you want. If it is not, then click on the AutoCorrect icon that appears by your text. You can then undo the automatic numbering just for this example, or disable the feature for future lists

1. Twelve grams of self-lowering flour

↶ Undo Automatic Numbering
   Stop Automatically Creating Numbered Lists
   Control AutoFormat Options...

From the Numbering pop-up menu choose Define New Number Format to fully customize the style, format and alignment.

3 Another way to create a numbered list is to enter your text with no numbers, then select it in the normal way and open the Numbering pop-up menu in the Paragraph section of the Home tab. As you hover over the different format options you'll see a preview of how your text will look if you chose that option

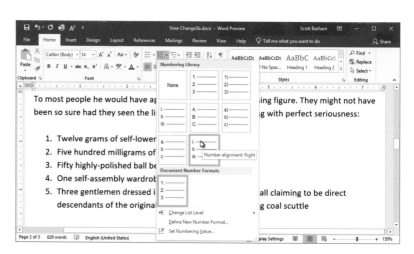

Multilevel lists

1 Create the text for your list. Press the Tab key at the beginning of a line once for each level of indent

2 Open the Multilevel pop-up menu in the Paragraph section and select the desired style

You can use the Change List Level option in the Multilevel pop-up menu to move an item to a higher or lower level. Alternatively, click at the beginning of a line and use Tab to move right or Shift + Tab to move left.

3 If you want to choose your own custom settings then select Define New Multilevel List

4 By clicking the Font button in this dialog you can control the appearance of the number at each level of the list, separately from the main text

You can also sort lists as text (alphabetic), numbers or by date. To do this, first select the list then click the sort icon in the Paragraph area of the Home tab.

Styles

Styles help you to apply a consistent set of formatting attributes to main text, headings and other elements of your document. Once you start using styles you'll be able to control your document's presentation with the minimum of tedious manual editing. Word comes with a set of styles for you to use straight away (in an area of the Home tab called the Styles Gallery), but it's also easy to create your own. There are two main types of style:

Paragraph styles

These can contain information about virtually any text attribute, e.g. font, size, alignment, spacing and color. They are called paragraph styles because they are applied at the paragraph level. In the Styles area paragraph styles are marked with a ¶ symbol.

Applying a paragraph style

A paragraph of text can only have a maximum of one paragraph style applied to it at any time. If you select a single word and apply a paragraph style to it, then the whole of the surrounding paragraph will be affected.

1 Choose the paragraph of text you want to format by clicking anywhere within it, or multiple paragraphs using any of the techniques covered in the previous chapter

2 If you hover over a style from the Styles Gallery in the Toolbar you'll see a preview of your text using the style. Choose one of the styles marked with a ¶ symbol. To see the full list of available styles, use the scroll bars or the ⊡ symbol in the bottom right of the Styles tools. Click once on the style to apply it to your text

There is a third type known as a Linked style. This can contain both character- and paragraph-level attributes. See page 54 for more about this.

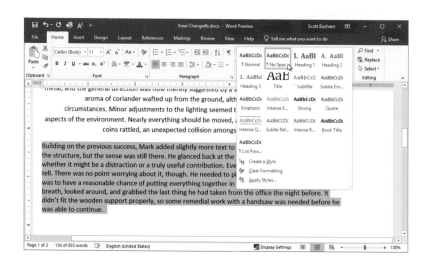

Character styles

These can contain information about character-level attributes only, e.g. font and size, but not alignment (which is a paragraph-level attribute). They can be applied to any amount of text, even individual characters or words. Character styles have no ¶ symbol.

Applying a character style

1 Select the text you want to change

2 Look for a style that doesn't have a ¶ symbol, and hover over it with the mouse. Your text will temporarily preview the selected style until you move off. Click directly on a style to apply it permanently to the selected text

It is very easy to accidentally override all your carefully-chosen text settings simply by clicking on a style in the toolbar. If this happens, choose Undo from the Quick Access Toolbar or press Ctrl + Z.

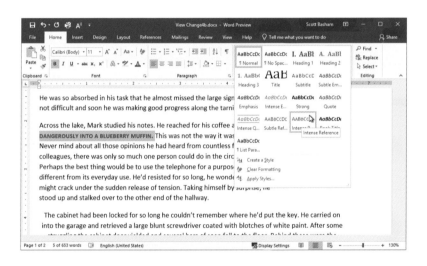

Removing the style from text

1 Select the text in question

2 Click the ⯆ symbol in the bottom right of the Styles tools to see the full list of styles plus a menu below these

3 Choose Clear Formatting to reset the text to a style called Normal. It's possible to redefine Normal to anything you like, as you will see in the next few pages

...cont'd

Creating a style

1 The easiest way to create a new style is to select some text that already has all, or most, of the attributes you want to use

2 Open the Styles panel by clicking the ⌐ icon in the lower right corner of the Styles area

You can also create a style directly from the palette of Styles in the extended panel, as seen in this illustration.

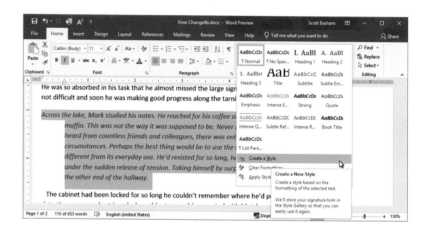

48

3 Click the New Style icon ☒ at the bottom of the panel

4 Note that the dialog shows you a preview of the style you're about to create. If this doesn't look correct then click the Cancel button and examine the text you selected. If necessary alter its formatting or select a different sample of text

You can apply a style to text using the keyboard shortcut Ctrl + Shift + S. An Apply Styles window will appear – type the first few letters of the style's name. If the desired style appears then click the Apply button; if not then select from the list.

5 If you're already happy with the style's attributes then click OK, otherwise select Modify to edit the settings

Modifying a style using the dialog box

1 Right-click the style in the Styles panel and select Modify

2 The following dialog appears. From here you can rename the style or alter attributes such as font, size, or effects including bold and italics

Many other useful settings can be made from this dialog. If you click the Format button, you can access dialogs for Font, Paragraph, Tabs and several other categories.

3 When you're happy with your settings, click OK. If there's any text in your document already using this style then it'll be automatically updated

...cont'd

Modifying a style using document text

One problem with modifying styles via the dialog box is that you don't see the results until you return to the main document. The following method doesn't suffer from this drawback:

1 Select text that already uses the style you plan to modify, and make the desired formatting changes

2 Right-click on the name in the Styles area and choose the "Update ... to Match Selection" option

Beware

When following these steps, make sure you click the right mouse button rather than the left. Left-clicking will reset the selected text to the original style definition. If you do this accidentally then use the Undo button, or Ctrl + Z, and try again.

Collapsing and expanding headings

This Word feature allows you to hide or reveal text below any headings that were formatted with the built-in styles.

1 Click the small triangle ▶ to the left of a heading

2 Click again to toggle the display of the contents On/Off

Hot tip

If your document is structured using multiple levels of heading (Heading 1, Heading 2, Heading 3, etc.) then collapse and expand can be used at each level to hide or reveal layers of detail in your text.

3 Editing in more depth

This chapter covers more advanced text editing including manipulation of styles, the Ruler, and using tabs to help with precision layout. It also covers some special effects, equations, and symbols.

The Styles panel

In the last chapter you started to use styles. You can create more advanced types of style from the Styles panel.

1 Open the Styles panel by clicking on the ⌐ icon in the bottom-right corner of the Styles area

2 You'll see a list of recommended styles

Hot tip

If you activate the Show Preview option, located at the bottom of the Styles panel, then the style names will appear using their own attributes.

Paragraph-level style

Character-level style

Blue underline char:
Font
    FONT 12 pt, Underline, Font color: Blue
Style
    Style Show in the Styles gallery, Priority: 2
Based on: Default Paragraph Font

Linked (Character- + Paragraph-level) style

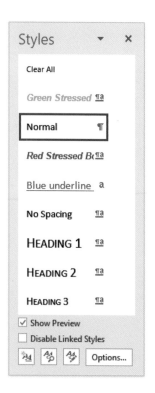

New Style   Style Inspector

Manage Styles

3 If you allow your mouse to hover over a particular style name, a summary box will appear. This lists the essential attributes of the style

4 Click on Options to select which styles should be shown in the Styles window. You can also control how they are displayed and sorted

Paragraph-level styles

Creating a new paragraph-level style

1 Make sure the Styles panel is open. If it isn't, click on the
⌐ icon in the bottom-right corner of the Styles area

2 Click the New Style button near the bottom

Don't forget

Paragraph styles are always applied to entire paragraphs. If you select just a few characters and apply a paragraph style then the whole of the surrounding paragraph will be affected.

53

3 Enter a style name, and choose a Style type of Paragraph

4 Select the other formatting options as appropriate. When you click OK your new style becomes available in the Styles area. Note the ¶ symbol next to its name

Linked styles

A linked style can be used at either the paragraph or the character level, depending on the amount of text selected when it's applied.

Creating a new linked style

1 Open the Styles panel by clicking the ▫ icon in the bottom right of the Styles area. Click the New Style icon

2 Give your style a name. For "Style type" select "Linked (paragraph and character)"

Try not to use too many effects if you have lots of small text, as they can make it unreadable.

3 Select the other formatting options as appropriate. In this example we've chosen green italic text with individual words underlined. You can set the word underline feature by clicking Format and choosing Font

4 Click OK when you're done. Your new style is now available. In the Styles panel the name is followed by a ¶a symbol to indicate it's a linked style

5 Select a whole paragraph of text (the quickest way to do this is to triple-click anywhere inside the paragraph), locate your new style in the Home tab and apply it

6 Now, select an individual word in a different paragraph and apply the style

7 To modify a style, click on the ⌄ symbol next to the style's name in the Styles panel and select Modify. Note that the style type setting is now grayed out. Once a style has been created as linked or character its type cannot be changed

Hot tip

Only a paragraph-level style can have its type changed. Although you can't change the others once created, you can always create a new style based on the existing one. To do this, simply select the style in the Styles panel then click the New Style button. You can now set the type for the new style.

Mixing styles in a paragraph

Character-level and paragraph-level styles can be used in the same paragraph. In this case, the character-level style's attributes take precedence. The following example is a good illustration of this.

1 Select an entire paragraph and apply a paragraph-level style to it. In this example, a style called "Green stressed body" was used. It's Arial, 10 point, green, italic, bold text

2 Now, select a small group of words within the paragraph and apply a character-level style. Here we've used a style called "Blue underline char style", which is 12 point, underlined and blue. The style definition has no font name built in so the font remains the same as that for "Green stressed body"

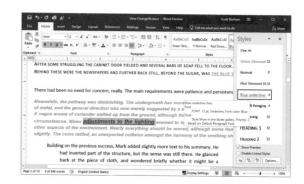

The selected words in this example still follow the attributes of the paragraph style, except where they have been overridden by the character-level style. So, if you edited "Green stressed body" to make its font Times New Roman, this would affect all the text. If, however, you made "Green stressed body" a darker green color, the text seen highlighted here would still be blue.

3 Note that the character-level style's attributes override those of the paragraph-level style

4 Now, with the same group of words selected, adjust the size to make it larger

5 Now, open the Styles window and click on the Style Inspector icon:

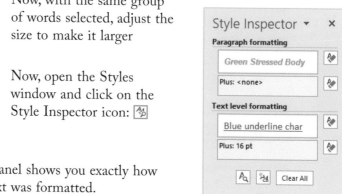

This panel shows you exactly how the text was formatted.

Using style sets

If you've been using Word's built-in styles, or if you've created your own by editing them and keeping the same names, then you can switch the style set to redesign your document completely.

1 Make sure the Design tab is active, and hover over a style set to see a preview of how your document would look

2 To see more options, click the ⊽ icon in the lower-right corner of the style set area. Select an option to make the change permanent

57

As your documents grow, you will want to check your formatting and overall design is consistent and easy to change, so make sure you use styles rather than formatting directly in the page.

3 Each style in the style set will replace the style of the same name in your current document. Any text that uses these styles will be automatically reformatted. This allows you to give even long documents a new and consistent design with the minimum of fuss

The horizontal Ruler can be displayed in most page views. However, the vertical Ruler displays in Print Layout view only.

You can change the measurements system from the File tab by choosing Options and then Advanced. In the Display section go to the option "Show measurements in units of:" and choose a different value. Points and Picas are sometimes useful as they match font sizes.

The Ruler

Text that is laid out neatly with accurate horizontal positioning greatly helps to give your documents a professional look. Effective use of white space, including tabulation, is the key to this.

Making the Ruler visible

1 Make sure that you are in Print Layout view. Activate the View tab and also make sure that the Ruler option in the Show area is active

Left indent for the first line of each paragraph

Left indent for subsequent lines

Drag here to move both left indents at once

Right indent

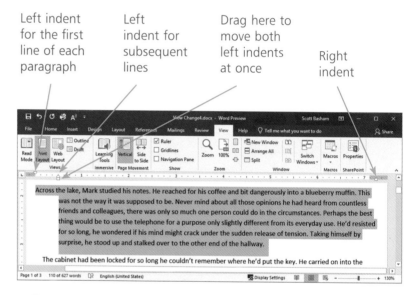

2 Experiment by moving the left and right indent markers on the Ruler and observe what happens on the page. It helps if you have several lines of text selected

Tabulation

Tab stops are paragraph-level attributes that define what happens if the Tab key is pressed when entering text. If you select a paragraph and examine the Ruler, you'll see any tab stops that have been defined. If no tab stops have been defined for this paragraph then the default tabs apply. These are marked in the Ruler as small vertical lines, spaced out at regular intervals in its lower section.

Overriding default tabulation

1 Click the Show/Hide ¶ button in the Paragraph section of the Home tab. This will allow you to see where you've pressed the Tab key – shown as a small arrow pointing to the right

2 Type in some text similar to the example below. Note that each text element is separated from the next by a tab character. Don't worry about how far across the screen the tab takes you – this will be altered soon. Make sure you only press Tab once between one element and the next

When you click the Show/Hide ¶ button, paragraph marks also appear visibly as the ¶ character.

3 Also, make sure that you press Return once at the end of each line. This will show up as a ¶ character as in the illustration above. The tab characters you entered display as right-pointing arrows

4 Now, select all the text you just entered. With the tabs in place you are ready to control exactly what they do

...cont'd

5 Make sure that the ⌐ icon is visible at the left side of the Ruler. This means that when you create a tab stop it will use left alignment. If it looks different, then click on it until it changes to the correct ⌐ symbol

6 Click in the Ruler around the 1-inch mark to create a new left tab. Drag it left or right to adjust its position

Hot tip

To see the distances between tab stops and the left and right indents, hold down the Alt key as you drag any of the Ruler icons horizontally.

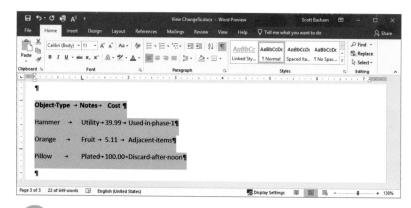

7 The characters should move so that the text following the first tab lines up vertically along its left edge. Making sure that your text is still selected, create some more tab stops. The text automatically moves to follow your new design

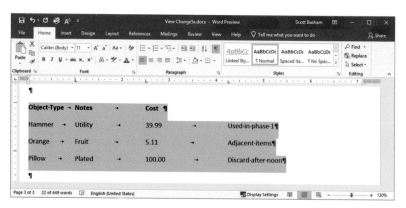

8 If you click at the end of the last line then press Return, you can add more lines using the same tab formatting

...cont'd

Different types of tabs

1 Keeping your text selected, delete the right-most tab by dragging it downwards from the Ruler until it disappears

2 Now, click on the └ symbol (at the very left edge of the Ruler) until it changes into a ⌐

3 Click in the Ruler near the right edge of the page. The text is moved so that it lines up along its right edge

When you click on the └ symbol, the icons cycle between left-, center-, right- and decimal-aligned tabs. After these there is the bar (vertical line) icon, followed by first-line indent and hanging indent icons.

4 If the text fails to align correctly then adjust the tab positions by dragging them left or right. Now call up the Tabs dialog by double-clicking directly on any tab

...cont'd

Don't forget

Tabulation can be built into a style definition, and so used consistently throughout a document.

5 Select a tab from the list. You can now change its type, add a leader (in the below example, we lead into the third tab with a line of dots), set new tabs, or clear tabs

6 In this example, bar tabs were created at 4 inches and 6 inches. These create vertical lines

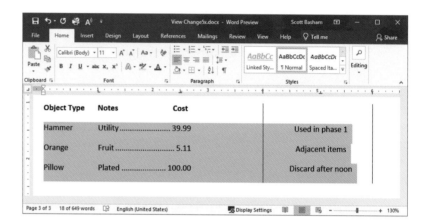

7 Sometimes the first line, since it contains headings, needs a slightly different form of alignment compared with the main text. In this example, the first line was selected on its own so that the word "Cost" could have a centered tab rather that the decimal tab with the leader of dots. Then the remaining lines were selected so that the formatting of the main text could continue

8 When you're done, click the Show/Hide ¶ button in the Paragraph section of the Home tab. This makes the hidden characters invisible again so that you get a better idea of the appearance of the final result

Hot tip

A decimal tab is useful for aligning numbers vertically so that their decimal point is in the same place.

Removing all tabs

1 Make sure all the relevant text is selected, then double-click on a tab to summon the Tabs dialog

2 Click Clear All, then OK

Editing controls

The right-hand side of the Home tab contains the Editing area with its Find, Replace and Select tools. These sometimes work in conjunction with the Navigation and Selection panes that you'll see later on.

The Find button

1 Press Ctrl + F or click the Find button in the Home tab. Click on its pop-up menu rather than the main part of the icon to see three options, one of which is Find

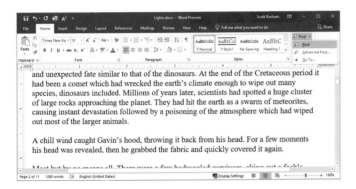

2 The Navigation pane appears along the left side of the screen. Enter your search text

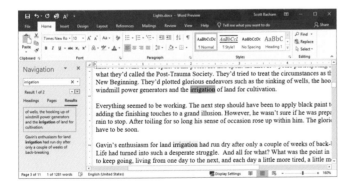

3 Word will immediately highlight all matches in the document, and also list them in the Navigation pane. If you scroll through these and click on an item in the Navigation pane, the main page will automatically move to that particular instance

Hot tip

If you click the pop-up menu icon (the small black triangle) next to the search text, you can ask Word to find other elements such as graphics, tables or equations. See Chapter 5 for more on pictures and graphics.

...cont'd

Advanced Find

Although the Navigation pane is useful for instant searches, you may want to use the Advanced Find feature to access more flexible and powerful options.

1 Open the pop-up menu next to the Find icon in the Editing area and choose Advanced Find

2 Click the More >> button to see the full set of options

3 Enter the search text in the "Find what" box

4 Note the option to match case – keeping this switched off means that searches are not case-sensitive

5 By clicking the Format button you can base your search on text attributes such as font or size. If you set some attributes and also enter text in the "Find what" box then Word will look for that particular text, but only if its attributes match what you've specified

6 To go ahead and run the search, click the Find In button and choose Main Document. If you happen to have selected some text within your document it's also possible to search just the selection

...cont'd

Find and Replace

Word can search through your document or selection, and substitute text, text attributes, or even a combination of the two.

1 To access the Find and Replace dialog you can either click directly on the Replace icon in the Editing area or use the keyboard shortcut Ctrl + H

Hot tip

You can also summon the Replace dialog box by using the pop-up menu in the Navigation pane, if available.

2 Enter the search text in the "Find what" area. While the cursor is still in this field you can also, optionally, click the Format button to specify search attributes

3 You can specify replacement text in the "Replace with" area. However, this example is a formatting change rather than a text substitution. In this case, ensure the cursor is in the "Replace with" box rather than "Find what" before clicking the Format button

...cont'd

The Replace function can make drastic changes to your document, particularly if you use the Replace All button.

4 You can now either use the Find Next and Replace buttons to check each substitution one at a time or, if you're confident to do it all at once, click Replace All

5 A message tells you how many changes were made. If this number worries you at all then use the Undo button (or Ctrl + Z) and then step through the changes one at a time with the Find Next and Replace buttons

6 In the above example, all instances of the word "irrigation" were made bold, red and underlined

Go To

The pop-up menu on the Find button in the Editing area has a Go To option that summons this dialog. It lets you jump easily to another document location, using a range of target options.

You can also access the Go To feature by using the pop-up menu in the Navigation pane, or with the keyboard shortcut Ctrl + G.

Using special characters

The Find and Replace dialog box also allows you to work with special characters such as paragraph markers or wildcards. It can even match words that sound similar to the search text.

 Choose Advanced Find and enter your search text. Click Special to see a list of special search characters

 In this example we selected "Any Digit" twice to insert the special code "^#" into the "Find what" box. The pattern "20^#^#" tells Word to look for the literal text "20" followed immediately by any two digits. As you can see in the yellow highlight, it has found "2011", "2012" and two instances of "2019"

Hot tip

If you activate the "Use wildcards" checkbox then the Special pop-up menu offers further options that can help make your searches very powerful. The illustration on the left shows both versions of the menu.

Advanced text effects

WordArt lets you present text using a wide range of visual effects.

Using WordArt

1 Select your text and then click on the WordArt icon in the Text area of the Insert tab

Don't forget

Initially the new WordArt object is independent of the main text, so you can easily move it by dragging. You can make it part of the main text by selecting it, clicking on its Text Wrap icon that appears on the right side, then selecting "In Line with Text".

2 Choose an effect from the gallery

Whenever your WordArt object is selected, the Drawing Tools Format tab is displayed. This can be used to customize its appearance further.

3 There's a set of WordArt tools in the Drawing Tools/Format tab. Click on the ⌐ symbol in WordArt Styles

4 Select or change an option to see the results in your document. You can resize the text box for the new object by dragging on its corner handles, or rotate using the top handle

If you spend a lot of time creating an effect, consider saving the result to the Quick Part Gallery – see page 85 in the next chapter for details on how to do this.

Creating a Drop Cap

1 Click anywhere inside a paragraph, then from the Text area on the Insert tab, click on the Drop Cap tool to select a Drop Cap style

2 The first letter becomes an object that can be resized by dragging on its handles, or reformatted as text

Equations and symbols

Equation Symbol

Symbols

Creating and editing an equation

1 Click the Equation icon in the Symbols area of the Insert tab, and select one of the prebuilt equations, or choose Insert New Equation to enter one manually

2 The equation appears as a new object on the page

Hot tip

If you can find something similar to what you need then it's much easier to select an existing preset equation and edit it – compared with entering the whole thing manually.

3 The Equation Tools tab appears. This can be used to help you manually edit the equation using all the standard symbols

4 Click the Equation icon again to see the Ink Equation option near the bottom of its list of actions. This lets you write by hand, using the mouse, pen, or touchscreen. Word will interpret this and convert to an editable equation

Inserting a symbol

1 Click on the Symbol icon in the Symbols area of the Insert tab to open the pop-up menu

2 If the symbol you want is in the display of commonly-used items, simply click to insert, otherwise click on More Symbols for a larger selection

4 Structured documents

Now that we've examined a range of editing techniques, it's time to look at features that make it easier to work with longer, more structured documents. We'll use controls in the Insert, Design and Layout tabs.

The Pages tools

The Pages area, on the left-hand side of the Insert tab, has three controls for working with pages.

Adding a blank page

Normally, you don't need to do anything to add pages to your document – as you add text and other objects, Word automatically makes room for them by creating new pages as necessary. Sometimes, however, you may want to force Word to create a new blank page in a specific part of your document.

Note that in Web Layout view the concept of pages is very different, as the whole document will exist in a web browser as a single page. In this case, your new blank page will show up as a few blank lines.

72

1 Click the Blank Page icon to add a new blank page

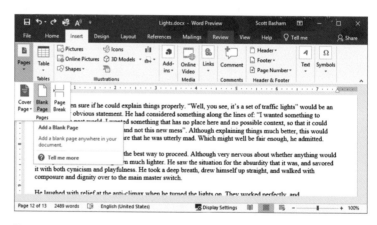

2 Any text before your insertion point will remain on its own before the new blank page. Any text after the insertion point will be moved to after the new blank page

You can repeat this process to add as many pages as you like. In this example, two pages have been inserted mid-way through the document.

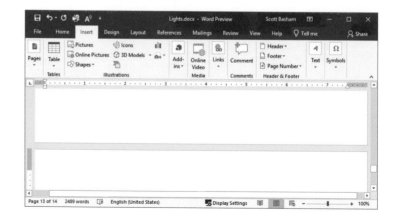

Adding a page break

1 Click the Page Break icon. Everything after the current cursor position will move to the next page

2 If the ¶ tool in the Home tab is active you'll be able to see the page break as a visible marker

When you're entering text you can type Ctrl + Return to insert a page break.

Like any other character, the page break can be selected and deleted if necessary.

Adding a cover page

1 Click the Cover Page icon and select from the gallery of styles available. The new page is inserted at the start

2 Select the placeholder text and type in your own

In this example, since you are replacing text, the original formatting is kept. This maintains the look and feel of the cover page design.

Tables and illustrations

These tools in the Insert tab allow you to add graphical elements to your document. As soon as you start working with tables or pictorial items, a new tab with relevant controls appears – this will be covered in detail in Chapter 5.

Always check to see which display mode you're using. If it's set to Draft or Outline then you will not see any graphical elements at all. For graphical editing work you should use the Print Layout view, available from the Status bar.

Print Layout

Icons and 3D Models are new to Word 2019, and are examined in more detail in the next chapter, Chapter 5 "Pictures and graphics".

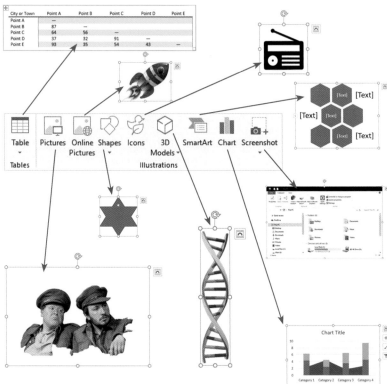

Note that some of the predesigned cover pages seen earlier contain graphical elements. If you use one of these it's possible to edit and format these pictorial components, just as if you'd added them yourself.

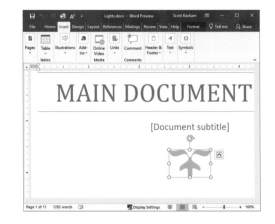

The Links tools

This section of the Insert tab lets you add links (hyperlinks), bookmarks, and cross-references.

Bookmarks

Defining bookmarks at key places in your document makes it easy to navigate to them, or even create hyperlinks from other areas.

Creating a bookmark

1 Navigate to the appropriate position in your document. Click on the Bookmark icon in the Links area

2 The Bookmark dialog appears. Enter a name for your bookmark and click on the Add button. Note that spaces are not allowed in the name

3 You can now use the Go To dialog to move instantly to a bookmark

The quickest way to get to the Go To dialog is to type Ctrl + G.

...cont'd

Links

A link, sometimes called a hyperlink, is usually presented as colored and/or underlined text. Clicking on a link will normally take you somewhere else – perhaps to a web page, a different document, or a different position within the current document.

Creating a hyperlink to a document on your computer

1 Place your insertion point wherever you want to add the hyperlink, or highlight the text to be hyperlinked

2 In the Links area of the Insert tab, click Link – or press Ctrl + K

This hyperlinking feature works in much the same way across all Microsoft Office applications.

3 For "Link to" choose "Existing File or Web Page" and locate the desired document. Select this and click OK

...cont'd

The hyperlink is inserted into your document. To follow it to its destination hold down the Ctrl key and click the link.

Hot tip

You can cross-refer to a range of possible targets including headings, bookmarks and tables.

Cross-references

Sometimes you'll want to refer to another location; e.g. "see page 89 for more information". If you actually type in the number "89" then you'll need to go back many times to check to see if that target reference has changed, perhaps because you've added more pages or edited some text. You can avoid this problem by creating automatic cross-references in Word.

1 Place your insertion point wherever you want the cross-reference to appear, then click the Cross-reference tool

Beware

When creating a cross-reference, click an insertion point rather than select text. This is because any text selected will be replaced by the cross-reference.

2 Choose the reference type and pick from the list of targets. Click Insert to see your reference

Hot tip

In the Cross-reference dialog you can also choose the form of the reference. For example, if your reference type is a heading you might want to use the heading number, the heading text itself, or the page number.

Headers and footers

Headers and footers appear at the top and bottom of each page. There are built-in items available with standard designs for these.

Adding a header or footer

1 In the Header & Footer area of the Insert tab click Header or Footer as appropriate

2 Select the design you want. The header or footer will be added to your document

Editing a header or footer

1 Double-click on the header or footer to enter edit mode. A new set of Header & Footer tools will appear

2 You will now be able to edit directly in the header or footer area of the page. With the Header & Footer tools you can adjust the position of the header and footer, add text or graphics, and even decide whether headers and footers should be separately defined for odd and even pages (this can be useful if you plan to print your document double-sided)

Hot tip

When you're finished working with headers and footers, simply double-click in the main page area to reactivate normal editing. Alternatively, click the "Close Header and Footer" button.

...cont'd

3 There is also a Navigation area in the tab, which allows you to switch between header and footer. If your document is divided into sections, then headers and footers can be defined independently for each section

See page 101 to learn how to divide your document into sections.

Inserting a date and time

1 Place your insertion point then click Date & Time

2 Choose from one of the formats listed then click OK

3 The current system date and/or time will be inserted at the current position

If you select the "Update automatically" option in this dialog then the date/time value is updated whenever the document is saved or printed.

The Text tools

These tools in the Insert tab let you add a variety of objects.

Text Boxes

These give you a lot of freedom in positioning and formatting small amounts of text. Text can also be flowed automatically between boxes, which can help with more advanced page layouts.

Using Text Boxes, Building Blocks and Quick Parts

1 Click the Text Box icon to access the pop-up menu

Text Boxes, like other shapes, can have text wrap applied to them. This is useful if you have a text-filled page – you can decide how the main text will flow around the edges of the Text Box. See page 120 for more on text wrap.

In the gallery that appears you'll see examples of Building Blocks. These are components that can be used in any document. You can define your own Building Blocks or download more from the **Office.com** resource. Other types of Building Blocks are headers, footers, page number styles, cover pages, watermarks, and equations.

2 If you hover over a design you'll see a tooltip with a brief explanation. Click on one of the designs to insert it into your current page

The Text Box appears on the page in whichever is the default position for this particular design.

3 To resize the Text Box, drag on one of its circular handles, either in the corner or halfway along each edge

As you drag an object, horizontal and vertical guides may appear. These are called alignment guides – see page 123 for more on how to activate these.

4 If you want to move the Text Box, then drag somewhere on its edge but not on any of its handles

5 The Text Box comes with some sample dummy text. Select this and enter your own

6 You can change the appearance of the text, or the box itself, using the controls in the Home tab or the Quick Access Toolbar

7 If you've enhanced or changed the design and would like to reuse it later on, make sure the Insert tab is active, click on the Quick Parts tool and choose "Save Selection to Quick Part Gallery". Name your design then click OK

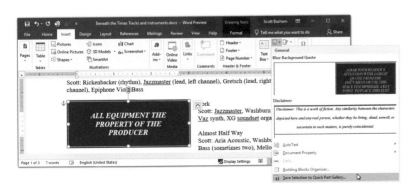

...cont'd

Creating a Text Box manually

1 Make sure the Insert tab is active. Click the Text Box icon and choose Draw Text Box

2 Your cursor will temporarily change to a cross. Drag a rectangular area to define the box perimeter

If you're not happy with the size of your Text Box you can either Undo and draw it again, or drag on its corner or edge handles to resize.

3 Click inside to enter the text within the box. You can use all the normal editing techniques and formatting controls you learned in earlier chapters

4 When the Text Box is selected, the Format tab will be available. You can use this to control the line and fill style of the box, as well as to change the layering (using "Bring to Front" and "Send to Back"). You can also apply more artistic effects such as shadowing, 3D boxes or geometric transformations

Sometimes the box may be too small for your text. If this happens you can either increase the box size, reduce the text size, or create more boxes and link them using text flow. We'll see how to use text flow next.

Flowing text between boxes

1 Locate a Text Box that has too much text to display within its defined area

Text flow works not just on Text Boxes, but on any shapes that are capable of containing text. See Chapter 5 for more details.

2 Click on the Text Box icon in the Toolbar and, in the pop-up menu that appears, choose Draw Text Box

3 Click and drag to define the second Text Box

4 Select the first Text Box and make sure the Format tab is visible. Click the Create Link button

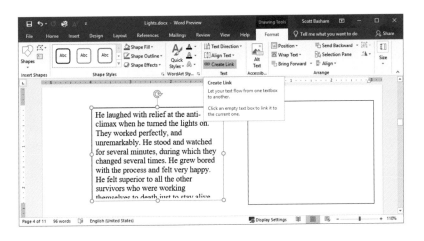

...cont'd

5 Now, click anywhere within the second Text Box. The text that didn't fit into the first box will automatically flow into the second

You can reverse this operation by selecting the first Text Box and then clicking on Break Link. All the text will be moved back into the first box. You will now need to edit the text, change its size, or change the size of the Text Box to see all the text once again.

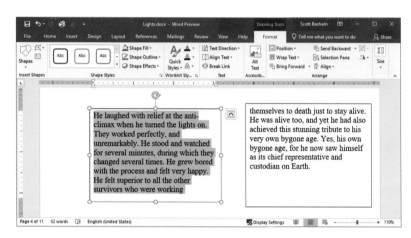

6 If there is still too much text, or if you decide to add more text, you can repeat this process to create a longer sequence of Text Boxes with the same text continuously threaded through them

7 The text remains linked, so changing the size and shape of any box will automatically cause the text to reflow. Similarly, adding or removing text may cause Word to readjust the flow between the boxes

...cont'd

Creating your own Building Blocks

As we saw on pages 80-81, you can select any text or other objects within Word and make these into new Building Blocks.

1 Create and format the content that will become your new Building Block

2 Select your content, then click Quick Parts and select "Save Selection to Quick Part Gallery"

Quick Parts are useful if you need to use standard formatted text across many documents. An example may be a disclaimer that has been agreed with the legal department of your company – it may be company policy to include this in any correspondence with customers.

3 The Create New Building Block dialog appears. Enter a name and select a gallery to use (in most cases this should be the Quick Part Gallery)

4 Choose a category and enter a text description

5 Next, choose the Word template that will store the Building Block. If you select "Building Blocks.dotx" then the Building Block will be available to all documents

6 The Options available are "Insert content only", "Insert content in its own paragraph", and "Insert content in its own page". Choose the appropriate option and then click OK. Your Building Block is now installed and ready for you to use from the Quick Parts tool

...cont'd

Using your own Building Blocks

Once you have created your own Building Blocks you can use them in the same way as the others.

1 Navigate to the part of your document where you want to add your Building Block, and click an insertion point

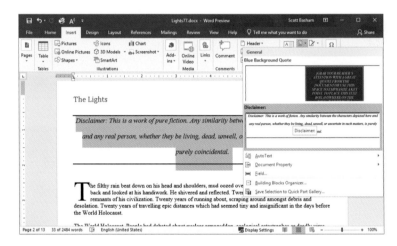

2 Click the Quick Parts button and select your Building Block from its gallery. It will be added at the current position

Editing an existing Building Block

If you have an example of a Building Block somewhere in your document, then you can edit this and reattach it to the gallery.

1 Make the necessary changes to the content, then select it

2 Click the Quick Parts button and make a careful note of the name of the Building Block you're planning to edit

3 Click on Quick Parts and choose "Save Selection to Quick Part Gallery"

4 If you enter exactly the same name and gallery as before then the original Building Block's definition will be overwritten

To replace an existing Building Block, you must enter precisely the same name in the Create New Building Block dialog.

The Building Blocks Organizer

Building Blocks can be very flexible, and there are many different types. In this chapter we have seen tools such as Cover Page, Header, Footer, Page Number, Text Box, and the more general Quick Parts. Each of these has its own gallery containing a particular type of Building Block. Here we'll see how to manage all these objects in one place.

1 Click on the Quick Parts tool and choose Building Blocks Organizer to see this dialog

The Quick Parts tool is in the Insert tab, as are most of the tools covered in this chapter.

2 If you scroll down through the predesigned elements you should be able to find Quick Parts objects you created yourself. Click Edit Properties to change an item's attributes

If you previously saved a customized text box as a Quick Part you might want to use this dialog to change its Gallery attribute to Text Boxes. It'll then appear directly in the pop-up menu that you see when you click on the Text Box tool.

Tables

Tables allow you to organize and manage text in rows and columns. They provide a more visual way of working than you'd have with normal text formatted via tab stops.

Inserting a table

1 Click on the Table icon in the Insert tab

2 In the grid that appears, click and drag to define an initial table size. Don't worry too much about getting this right first time, as it's easy to change the size later on

Hot tip

If you already have some text formatted using tab characters, then it's easy to convert this to a table automatically. To do this, select the text, click the Table icon and choose "Convert Text to Table".

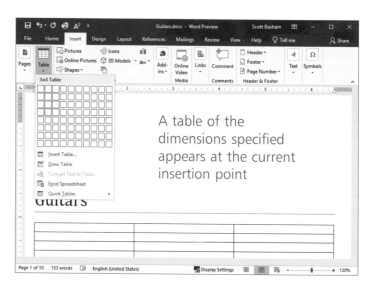

A table of the dimensions specified appears at the current insertion point

3 Alternatively, if you click the Table icon and then choose Insert Table from the sub-menu, this dialog box appears. You can then specify the table dimensions numerically. Click OK to go ahead and create the table

...cont'd

Resizing a table

1 Click and drag on the boundary between rows or columns to resize them. Your cursor will turn into a double-headed arrow as you do this

As soon as you have a table or part of a table selected, the Table Tools tab will appear. This is organized into two sub-tabs: Design, and Layout.

Drawing a table

You may prefer to use the table drawing tool to create tables. This gives you more flexibility, particularly when you're trying to create irregularly-shaped tables.

1 Click the Table icon and choose Draw Table

2 Click and drag to draw a rectangle that defines the overall table size

The rectangle you drew represents the table perimeter. Your next task is to draw in the rows and columns. The special Table Tools/Layout tab is automatically activated and its Draw Table tool is selected ready for you to start work.

...cont'd

3 Click and drag horizontally across the table to draw in the rows. As you drag, a dotted or red line appears, giving you a preview of the new line. If you accidentally draw the line in the wrong place, simply use Ctrl + Z to undo, and then try again

All these features are still available to you even after you add text into the cells of your table. Sometimes it's useful to see how much text you need before you finalize the table's dimensions.

4 Now, drag vertically to draw in the column boundaries

5 You can even drag diagonally to create a new line that will divide cells in two, as in the example below

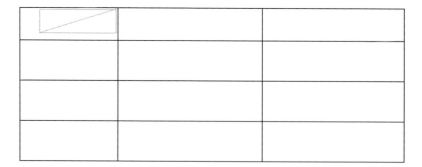

Note that if you drag from inside to an area outside of the table, then nothing will be changed. However, if you begin and end dragging completely outside the table, then a new independent table will be created.

6 Sometimes you will want to remove lines to create an irregular table where some of the cells are much larger. To do this, select the Eraser tool and then click directly on the part of the line you wish to remove

A single click will normally remove the shortest segment at the current mouse position. If you want to remove larger sections of a line, or even a whole line, then click and drag over the desired area.

7 Once you have erased a fairly large area, switch back to the Draw Table tool. You can now add in more lines to this area

8 In the example below you can see how flexible this technique is, allowing for a complex patchwork of odd-sized cells to be created

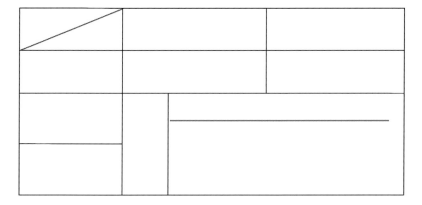

Table cells are normally filled with text, and can have their background shaded and different line styles applied. It's also possible to place other items such as graphics inside a table cell.

Hot tip

If you have changed the dimensions of individual rows or columns, but now want to make your table more regular again, then select the relevant area, right-click and choose either Distribute Rows Evenly or Distribute Columns Evenly.

...cont'd

Formatting your table

You can use all the formatting techniques learned in earlier chapters on your table text. Often you'll start by dragging across an entire row or column to select it prior to formatting.

Guitars

Name	Type	Price
Rickenl	ctric	$1871.00
Epipho		$499.99
Squire		$283.65

Calibri (B ▾ 14 ▾ A˄ A˅ ☰ ▾ ☰ ▾ ▦ ▾ ▤ ▾ Insert Delete
B I ☰ ab ▾ A ▾ ◌ ▾ ▦ ▾ ✦

Bold (Ctrl+B)

Inserting and deleting rows or columns

1 To insert a row, first select an existing row just above or below where you want it to be

2 To the left of the row, a circular icon with a plus sign inside will appear as you hover over with the mouse. Click this icon, and the new row will be inserted

Guitars

Name	Type	Price
Rickenbacker 330	Hollow Body Electric	$1871.00
Epiphone Viola	Bass	$499.99
Squire Telecaster	Solid Electric	$283.65

3 To insert additional rows, keep clicking on the icon

4 To add multiple rows in a single action, first click and drag to select the number of rows you wish to add. When you click the circular icon, Word will add the same number of rows

5 You can add columns in a similar way. Select one or more columns then move your mouse to the top left or top right of the area you've selected. The circular Add icon will appear, allowing you to add in the columns

Merging cells

Each cell can contain text that is formatted and aligned independently of other cell text (if desired). Sometimes it's useful to group or merge cells together so that they behave as a single cell.

1 Select the cells you wish to merge. Note that these must be next to each other

2 Right-click and choose Merge Cells

If you accidentally merge the wrong cells then type Ctrl + Z or click on the Undo button in the Quick Access Toolbar.

93

Your selected area will now be a single cell. All the text that was in the original cells will be present in the new cell.

3 Select the new cell, then make sure the Layout tab in the Table Tools is active. In the Alignment area choose Align Center. Note that the centering acts across the whole area, so it really is behaving as if it was a single cell

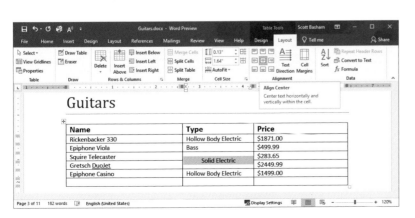

...cont'd

Table Properties

Hot tip

From the Cell tab of the Table Properties dialog you have individual control over the vertical alignment of text within each cell. Horizontal text alignment can be controlled via the Paragraph area in the Home tab, or both together from the Alignment area of the Table Tools Layout tab.

1 Make sure your insertion point is somewhere inside the table (or select part or all of the table), right-click and then choose Table Properties

From this dialog you can define properties for the entire table, or at the row, column, or cell level.

You can also use the "Borders and Shading" button to set the visual properties for the whole table.

Table Styles

1 Select or click within your table to make sure the Table Tools tab is active. Make sure the Design sub-tab is selected, and look for the area named Table Styles. As you hover over each style you'll see a preview of your table

2 Click on the style to apply it permanently to your table

Hot tip

Word includes a wide selection of preset table styles, helping you to quickly apply an effective design without spending hours fiddling with formatting settings.

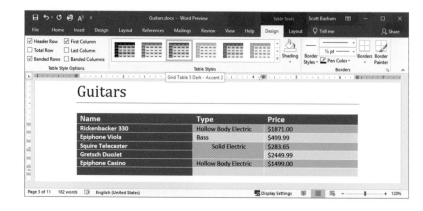

The Table Design controls

1 Click anywhere in your table and make sure the Table Tools Design tab is active

2 Select one or more cells to apply background colors via the Shading icon

3 Choose a Border Style to activate the Border Painter. This turns your cursor into a paintbrush that you can use to change the border style of any lines in your table

The Table Layout controls

If you activate the Layout controls you'll see that there are tools for operations on tables, rows, columns, and individual cells.

In this example, the Formula button was used to calculate the sum of the values in the cells above the one selected.

Hot tip

Many of the features in the Table Layout controls are also present in the pop-up menu when you right-click within a table.

Themes

Themes can control your overall document design by defining its main colors, fonts and effects. If you use a Theme's colors, for example, then changing the Theme will change these automatically.

Selecting a Theme

1 Make sure the Design tab is active

If your current document does not use Theme fonts, colors and effects then applying a new Theme will have no visible effect. To remedy this, whenever you choose a font, color or effect, make sure you use an option that is listed under Theme.

2 Click the Themes button and browse through the Themes in the Gallery. As you hover over a Theme, your document will preview its settings. Click once to set the Theme

3 All aspects of the document under Theme control will be updated to reflect your choice

Using a Theme's colors

1 To change just the colors that belong to the Theme, click on the Theme Colors icon in the Design tab. A gallery of color swatches appears

2 Choose a different option. If your document used Theme colors then these will be changed automatically

3 From now on, whenever you select a color you will be able to choose one from the Theme's current selection

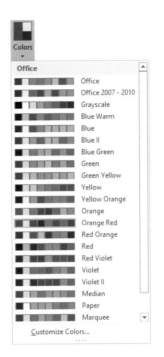

Using a Theme's effects

1 You can also change a Theme's effects independently of its fonts and colors. To do this, click on the Effects button in the Design tab and select a different option. As you hover over an option, the effect will be previewed

...cont'd

Using a Theme's fonts

1 Make sure the Design tab is active, then click on Fonts in the Document Formatting area. Each option contains one font for headings, and a second for main body text

2 Choose a different option. If your document used Theme fonts then these will be changed automatically

Hot tip

As you hover over an option, any text currently using Theme fonts will preview the new settings.

3 Now, switch back to the Home tab and open the Fonts menu. At the top you will see the two Theme fonts. If you carry out more of your formatting using these, you can easily switch Themes later – your text will change accordingly

4 It's a very good idea to make sure your text styles are defined using Theme fonts – if your document uses those styles throughout, then it's very easy to experiment with different designs

Page Setup

This set of tools includes controls for margins, size and orientation, as well as line numbering, adding breaks, and hyphenation.

Margins and columns

1 Make sure that the Layout tab is active. In the Page Setup area click on the Margins icon to choose from the Gallery, or click Custom Margins to define these via a dialog box

2 By default, your text is set out in a single column spread across the page. To change to a multi-column layout, click the Columns icon and choose the number you want. Your text will be reformatted in the new layout

For this example make sure you choose the Breaks tool present in the Layout tab (and not Page Break from the Insert tab).

Don't forget

The quickest way to add a simple page break is to press Ctrl + Return.

Don't forget

The Columns control is also found in the Page Setup area of the Layout tab.

Breaks

Different types of break

At the start of this chapter we saw how to add a simple page break. The Layout tab also has a tool for this, but it's much more powerful.

1 Position your insertion point then click the Breaks tool

2 As you can see, there's a number of different options. To help organize our document we'll create a section break – choose the Continuous type

3 At first sight nothing seems to change. However, if you click on the ¶ tool in the Home tab you'll see the break

4 Now, click in the text after the break and change the number of columns. Note that this affects just the current section; i.e. the text after the break

5 If you add more section breaks to your document, then you'll be able to set columns for each section separately

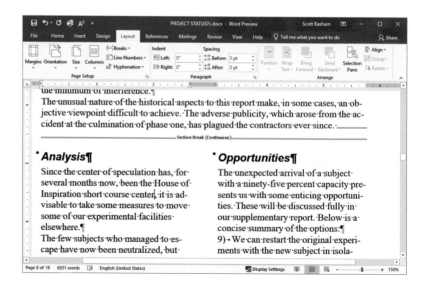

Sections

Dividing a document into sections

It's useful to divide your document into sections using the Next Page section break, so that the next section starts on a new page. This helps organize your work, and different sections can have their own page numbering, plus different headers and footers.

1 Divide your document into sections by clicking the Breaks tool and choosing a Next Page section break. On the first page after a section break, double-click anywhere within the footer to see the Header and Footer tools

2 Click the "Link to Previous" icon (in the Navigation area of the Design tab) to deactivate it. You can now set a different footer for this section

3 If you have an automatic page number, then right-click on it and choose Format Page Numbers

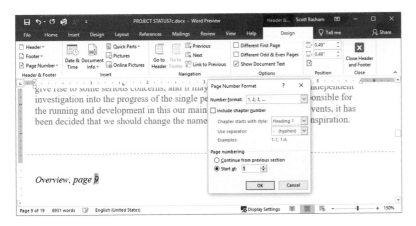

4 Change the Page Numbering option to restart at page 1

Hot tip

It's worth spending some time customizing each section. In this example, the footer text in the new section has been changed. The document's earlier footer used the text "Overview", but for this section it's changed to "Essential Information".

...cont'd

Line numbers

You can add line numbers to your whole document or to sections, and you can also switch this on and off for individual paragraphs.

1 Either select your whole document or just click within a section, depending on where you'd like line numbering

2 Click on Line Numbers and select an option

The Layout tab also reproduces the indent and spacing settings that are available in the Paragraph dialog (accessible from the Home tab). The dialog itself can also be summoned using the icon in the lower-right corner.

The Page Setup dialog

1 Click on the small icon in the lower-right corner of the Page Setup tools area

2 This dialog contains controls for adjusting the margins and page orientation, as well as advanced settings for setting multiple pages per printed sheet

If your screen doesn't match this illustration then make sure the Margins tab within the dialog is active.

...cont'd

3 Click the Paper tab to define the size and printing options

4 The Layout tab lets you make settings for either the whole document or individual sections. You can also access line numbering and border options

Hyphenation

Word can automatically hyphenate your text for you. This can allow more text to fit on the page, particularly useful if lines of text are not very long. You can also choose manual hyphenation, where Word will prompt you for each potential instance. Hyphenation can be appropriate when working with a layout that uses many columns, such as a magazine or newspaper design.

Hot tip

Click the Hyphenation tool and choose Hyphenation Options to see the following dialog. This gives you finer control over exactly how much hyphenation takes place.

With automatic hyphenation, Word uses special information in its dictionary to decide where within a word a hyphen can be placed. This dictionary is specific to each installed language used by Word.

Page background

These controls can be found at the right side of the Design tab.

Watermark

You can add either a text or a picture watermark using the Watermark tool. This will appear as a background to the page, and can be lightened so that it does not dominate too much.

Page color

Using the Page Color tool you can set your page to a solid color, or even a graduated fill. This can be a good option if your document is to be read online, but is perhaps best avoided when printing, due to the amount of ink required.

Page borders

You can add a range of borders to the edges of your page.

1 Click on the Page Borders icon in the Design tab

The Shading tab in this dialog allows you to apply a background shading to the current paragraph.

2 Choose your setting and experiment with the line style, color, and width. The Art pop-up lets you select from a range of graphic designs. As you work, the Preview section on the right will give you some visual feedback

3 You can choose different borders for different sections, or apply a border to the whole document as in this example

5 Pictures and graphics

This chapter looks at Word's graphical features, from photos and video through to charts, diagrams, icons, 3D models and screenshots.

Pictures

The Illustrations area

The Illustrations area of the Insert tab allows you to add a range of different graphical objects.

Don't forget

Word can import many types of graphic file format, and these fall into two main categories: draw-type graphics are represented as mathematical objects. They can usually be scaled up or down with no loss in quality. The other type is bitmapped; i.e. stored as a structure of dots or pixels. Be careful not to enlarge bitmapped images too much, as the pixels get bigger and more noticeable.

Adding a photo from a file on disk

In this example we'll import an image created by a digital camera. We'll assume that we have some photo files available on the hard disk or other storage medium.

1 Navigate to the appropriate part of your document, then click on Pictures in the Illustrations area of the Insert tab

2 Use the standard Windows controls at the top and the left of the dialog to locate the photo files

Hot tip

If you move your mouse over one of the images you'll see some additional file details.

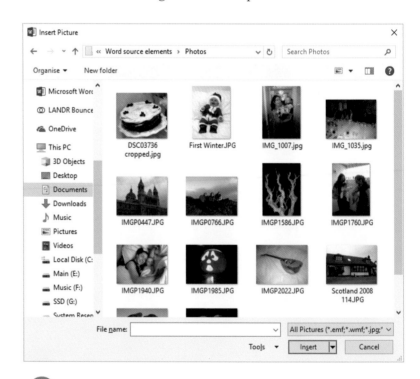

3 Once you have found the image you want, select it and then click the Insert button

...cont'd

4 The image is brought into the current page. Note that it has eight circular "handles", which can be dragged around if you want to manipulate the image

Don't forget

Drag the circular arrow icon to rotate the image; any other handle will resize it

Drag directly on an edge (not on a handle) to move without resizing

Drag on a corner handle to resize, keeping the picture in proportion. Drag on one of the handles halfway along an edge to stretch just vertically or horizontally.

5 Sometimes you'll want to cut away unnecessary parts of the picture. Click on the Crop tool and you'll see some heavy black corners and edges. Dragging inwards on these will prepare the image for cropping

Hot tip

6 When you're happy with your adjustments, click on the Crop tool again and choose Crop to apply the changes. If you change your mind later, simply reselect Crop and drag the black handles outwards again

In the Crop tool's pop-up menu there are also options to "Crop to Shape", and many preset shapes to choose from.

...cont'd

Remove background

If your photo has a prominent main object that is easily distinguishable from its background, then you can get help from Word to remove the background automatically.

1 Select the photo, then click the Remove Background tool in the Adjust area of the Picture Tools Format tab

The Picture Tools Format tab only appears when a picture is selected in your document.

2 The magenta-colored area indicates Word's guess at what is the background. If it hasn't got it quite right, then use the "Mark Areas to Keep" and "Mark Areas to Remove" tools to subtract from or add to the magenta area

...cont'd

3 When you're satisfied that the correct area is defined, click the Keep Changes icon and the background will be removed

Most of the tools described here are in the Picture Tools/Format tab. If you select a picture, the tab, although available, may not be currently active. In this case, simply click on the tab title (depicted below) to select it.

Artistic Effects

Although Word isn't a fully-blown photo manipulation package, it does have a range of tools for both creative and corrective work.

1 Select the photo and click the Artistic Effects tool

2 The pop-up menu contains options for treating your photo using creative filter effects, as you can see in this example. Hover over an option to see a live preview

Similar to Artistic Effects the Corrections tool, gives you a number of options for sharpening/ softening and for adjusting brightness and contrast of a photo.

...cont'd

The Adjust tools
There are some useful tools in the Adjust area of the Picture Tools/Format tab, although three might not have visible captions:

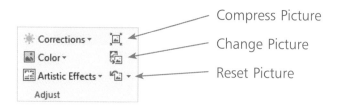

Compress Picture

Change Picture

Reset Picture

Compress Picture gives you the opportunity to reduce the file size used for your image (and consequently reduce upload and download time if copying across the web or via email). You can do this by permanently removing cropped-out areas, or by changing the detail level (resolution).

Change Picture lets you substitute in a new picture file, whilst preserving the attributes such as size and crop information.

Reset Picture removes all the formatting, effectively returning the image to how it was when first imported.

Picture styles
The Quick Styles icon in the Picture Styles area lets you easily apply a wide range of visually-interesting effects such as shadow, glow, reflection, rotation or a combination of these in a preset style.

The Format Picture pane

As well as the tools in the Format tab, there is a task pane window that gives you more control over your picture settings.

1 Select the photo and click the Picture Styles ▣ icon

2 The Format Picture task pane will appear. Make sure the Shadow tools are active to see the controls available

3 Scroll down the Format Picture pane to see the range of other controls. Use the small, white or black triangles to reveal and hide settings

The Format task pane's controls will change to reflect what is currently selected. If, for example, you select some text, it then turns into a Format Text Effects panel.

Side panels can be undocked by dragging on their title away from the current position. Once free from the main window, they can be positioned and resized easily. To re-dock, simply drag onto the left or right side of the tabbed controls area.

...cont'd

Pictures

Adding a draw-type picture from a file on disk
In this example we'll import and manipulate a draw-type object.

1 Navigate to the appropriate part of your document, then click on Pictures in the Illustrations area of the Insert tab

2 Once you've found a suitable draw-type graphic, select it and then click the Insert button

Don't forget

Draw-type graphics can generally be edited with no appreciable loss in quality, as they are stored as a set of mathematical objects. Using the Online Pictures button (see page 114), try searching for ClipArt with "WMF" in the search criteria. This stands for Windows MetaFile, and is a widely-used standard for draw-type graphics.

3 If the graphic consists of a number of shapes, then it's usually possible to edit its individual components. To do this, right-click to access the pop-up menu. Click on Group to see a sub-menu, and select Ungroup

Hot tip

You can also convert an imported draw-type picture by right-clicking on it and choosing Edit Picture.

4 If you see the dialog box pictured above, click Yes

5 Often this will be sufficient for you to start editing individual elements. Experiment by clicking on different areas of the graphic to see what you can select. Once an element is selected it can usually be moved, resized, rotated, or formatted using different colors or line styles

Paint-type graphics cannot be manipulated in this way. They are represented as a grid of rectangular pixels (picture cells) rather than objects, and so cannot be broken down into simpler elements.

6 Sometimes a draw-type graphic consists of items that are grouped together. If it does, you can break it down further by right-clicking and choosing Grouping and then Ungroup

7 The graphic is now split into a set of smaller objects

The easiest way to select all the objects within the general graphics frame is to click on one (to establish selection within the frame), then type Ctrl + A for Select All.

8 Experiment by editing one or two objects. You can use the Format tab to apply new borders, color or styles

9 When you've finished you might want to regroup. To do this, select all the objects then right-click, choose Group and select Group again from the sub-menu

Converted draw-type graphics "live" inside a rectangular frame area. It is sometimes a good idea to drag on one of its circular edges or corner handles to make it larger. This gives you more room in which to move and edit elements.

Online
Pictures

Online pictures

1 Move your insertion point to the place in your document where you'd like to put the picture

2 Go to the Insert tab, and click the Online Pictures icon

Beware

Some online pictures are subject to copyright restrictions – you can check for these by clicking on the blue links in the dialogs shown here. In many cases you are free to use the photograph, but you may be required to credit the author in a caption. Word has automatically added an editable caption in the below example.

3 You can either select from the categories available or enter some search text in the dialog that appears. When you've found a suitable picture select it then click on the Insert button

This Photo by Unknown Author is licensed under CC BY-SA

4 The picture is imported into the current position. It can now be manipulated just like other photos

114

Shapes

Word offers a large selection of standard graphic shapes that can be drawn and then customized.

1 Click on the Shapes icon in the Insert tab. A gallery of standard shapes appears. These are draw-type graphics so you can resize and manipulate them in many ways without loss in quality

2 Select one of these. This example uses "Down Arrow Callout"

3 Click and drag diagonally to create the initial shape. If it's the wrong size or position this can be changed easily

Shapes

Don't forget

You can rotate Shapes just like other graphic elements by dragging on the circular arrow tool that appears above the item when it's selected.

Adjust box height
Adjust shaft width
Adjust arrow length
Adjust arrow width

4 You can move the object by dragging directly on it. Drag on a white circular handle (corner or edge) to resize it

5 Drag on a yellow circular handle to change a single aspect of the shape. Precisely what this changes depends on the shape, so it's worth experimenting. In the above example the yellow handles let you customize the dimensions of the box and the arrow part individually

Hot tip

Right-click on a shape and choose Edit Points. You'll then be able to change the shape by dragging its vertices. Click and drag along a line to add a new point. Right-click a point to choose between Smooth, Straight or Corner.

3D Models

Here we'll see how you can import and even manipulate 3D objects within your Word documents.

1 Click on the 3D Models icon in the Insert tab and select either "From a File" or "From Online Sources"

2 In this example we are selecting from Online Sources. Choose a category to see the options available or, alternatively, enter some text in the Search box and click the magnifying glass icon

3D Model import is a new feature added with Word 2019.

Word can import 3D Models from the following file formats: Filmbox (*.fbx); Object (*.obj); 3D Manufacturing (*.3mf); Polygon (*.ply); StereoLithography (*.stl); and Binary GL Transmission (*.glb).

3 When you have selected the desired 3D graphic, click the Insert button. You may have to wait for a few moments while Word processes the file

...cont'd

Your 3D graphic will appear at the current document position. You can move, resize and use the normal rotation tool just as you can for ordinary graphic elements

Choose from the 3D Model Views area to jump straight to one of its main views

Drag directly on this icon to control 3D rotation

In the center of the graphic is a special 3D rotation tool. If you drag on this you can rotate the graphic about its other two axes. By using this in combination with the normal rotation tool you can turn the model in any direction you like. In the example below we made six copies of our dinosaur so that we could compare different rotational views

Hot tip

When you have a 3D object selected, the Format tab shows two extra tools. 3D Models lets you import another graphic, while Reset 3D Model will switch it back to its initial view and (optionally) change it back to its initial size.

Icons

Insert an Icon

Insert an icon to visually communicate using symbols.

Icons are usually simple bold graphics used to convey a concept in a visually-striking way, independent of language.

1 To add an icon to your document, first make sure the Insert tab is active and click on Icons. The following dialog box appears

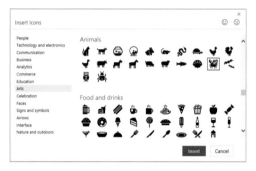

2 Select a category from the list on the left, and then browse through the available icons

3 Select your icon then click the Insert button

4 The icon will appear at the current position in your document. It can be moved and sized just like any normal graphic. Because it is a draw-type graphic, it can also be edited further. To do this, right-click on the icon and choose "Convert to Shape"

Icon import is another new feature added with Word 2019.

5 Click Yes to the following dialog

6 Now that the icon has been converted, you can right-click and choose **Edit Points** from the pop-up menu

7 The shape can now be manipulated as a set of straight lines and curves connecting points that are marked as black squares. If you select one of these you can adjust curvature by dragging on the white square "handles" that appear

8 You can apply other object effects such as Shape Fill and Outline from the Drawing Tools/Format tab

Because icons are drawing objects you can perform actions such as resizing, rotating, and scaling without any loss in quality.

Layout options

1 Select any object and then click on the Layout Options icon to see the following settings

The Layout Options icon appears at the top right of any object you select, and provides a quick way of controlling how it interacts with its surroundings.

2 If your object overlaps text, you may be interested in using text wrap. "Tight" is sometimes all you need for surrounding text to closely follow the shape's contours

3 Right-click on the object and a menu will appear. Choose Wrap Text then Edit Wrap Points. You'll then see the text wrap border defined as straight black lines connected by small black squares that work as handles

The Arrange tools on the right of the Format tab can be used to align objects, and move them in front of or behind other objects.

4 Drag one of these handles to move the boundary line. If there's text nearby then you'll see it move so that it's always outside the perimeter

To delete a text wrap handle, hold down the Ctrl key and click directly on the handle.

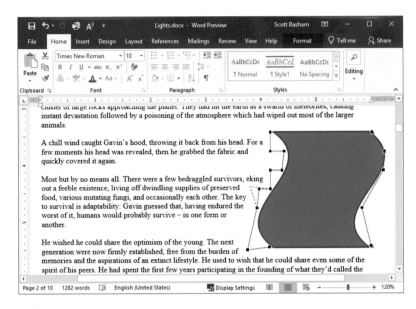

5 Click and drag on the border, but not on an existing handle, to create a new handle. Using these controls you can alter the way text flows around any irregular shape

6 Click on an object's Layout Options icon and choose "See more" to see a dialog where you can numerically set position, text wrap, and size. Some of these options are also available from the Layout and Format tabs

...cont'd

Adding text inside a shape

Most shapes can be used as Text Boxes, and all the normal text formatting options are available within these.

1 If there's currently no text in the shape, then right-click and choose Add Text

2 Enter the text (or paste from the Clipboard)

3 Format using the Mini Toolbar or the other tools

4 You can still apply effects to the shape itself. If you rotate, for example, the text will rotate as well (when you edit the text it will temporarily switch back to horizontal so you can easily read what you are trying to change)

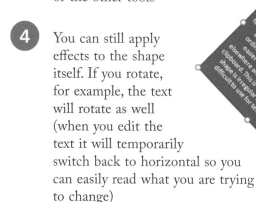

Canvas objects

When you ungroup a complex object it will, by default, become a series of smaller items within a rectangular canvas object. You can move the whole thing or set layout options by clicking on the canvas border, or manipulate the individual items inside by selecting them in the normal way.

Don't forget

It's usually worth resizing the canvas object to make it larger. Make sure you give yourself enough room to easily manipulate the graphic objects within. You can always shrink the canvas again later.

Resize canvas object here

Select canvas object here

Click here for individual smaller objects within

Controlling layout

Alignment guides

1 Go to the Layout tab, click Align and make sure Use Alignment Guides is selected

2 Move an object to see temporary vertical and horizontal guides – these assist with alignment to other objects

Hot tip

The alignment guides are magnetic and so help you to easily align the object you're moving with other items such as margins, graphics, or the center of the page.

Live layout

Word gives you a real-time preview of your document as you move, resize, or rotate a picture – so you can see exactly the effect of your changes without any delay.

Online video

As long as your computer is online, you can easily add video to your documents from a variety of sources.

1 Click Online Video in the Media area of the Insert tab

Websites showing online video sometimes have controls that display the relevant embed code, which you can copy and paste into the bottom section of the Insert Video dialog.

2 The Insert Video dialog appears. Either enter some text to search YouTube or enter a video embed code directly

Word does not actually embed the video in the document – instead, it stores a link to its source website. This keeps your documents small, but it also means that you need to be online whenever you attempt to play the video.

3 Select the video then click the Insert button. The Video object is added to the current location. You can move, resize, or play it by clicking the white triangle

SmartArt

SmartArt graphic items allow you to present concepts and information in a visual way.

SmartArt

1 Click on the SmartArt icon in the Insert tab. The following dialog appears. Choose an item and click OK

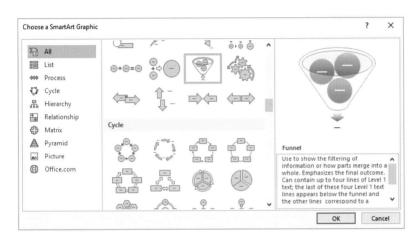

2 Click on Text Pane in the Create Graphic area of the Design tab to make it visible. Enter your text in the window on the left, and it will appear in the diagram

Hot tip

You can radically change your design at any time by changing the selection from the Layouts and SmartArt Styles in the Design tab.

3 You can work on parts of the object by selecting individual items and then formatting, moving, resizing, or performing other types of edit

...cont'd

The SmartArt tools

Whenever SmartArt objects are selected, the SmartArt Tools appear, divided into two tabs: Design and Format.

1 In the Design tab make sure the Text pane is activated by clicking on the icon. Use the Create Graphic controls to promote/demote the text lines, or Tab to indent directly

SmartArt objects are ways of presenting text lists in graphical form. Often you'll edit the text directly on the object, but sometimes it's more useful to view and change it in the separate Text pane.

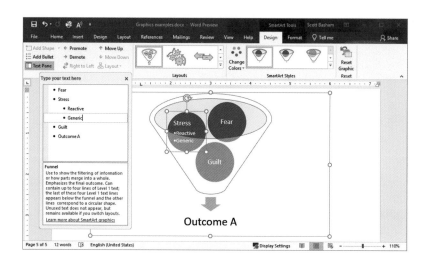

2 Activate the Format tab to experiment with different visual effects

Depending on what you select, these Format controls can apply to the whole object or to individual parts.

Charts

If you've used Microsoft Excel you may be familiar with the concept of presenting tables of figures in chart form.

Chart

1 Click on the Chart icon in the Insert tab. The following dialog appears, with a large selection of chart variants

2 Choose a chart type and click OK

Don't forget

If you don't like the chart type you selected it's easy to go back and select another, so enjoy the freedom to experiment.

3 A default chart appears. You can select and customize this using the Chart Tools tab, which appears automatically

Hot tip

If Excel is installed on your computer, you can click the 📊 "Edit Data in Microsoft Excel" button to access its full range of features.

4 A separate window opens, displaying some sample chart data. You can edit this so that the chart uses your own text and figures

Screenshots

Many technical and training documents make use of screenshots. These are images taken directly from the computer screen, perhaps demonstrating a particular task within a program. Some people use the PrtScn key, which places an image of the entire current screen in the Clipboard (Alt + PrtScn snapshots just the currently-selected window). Since this functionality is rather limited, others might use special utility software. However, there's also support for doing this directly within Word.

1 Click the Screenshot icon in the Insert tab. The pop-up will show you the thumbnails of the current windows – either choose one of these or select Screen Clipping

Hot tip

If you choose Screen Clipping then you'll be able to click and drag to define a rectangular area to crop within the screen display area.

2 The screenshot is inserted as a picture into your document. Note this is a bitmap (rather than a draw-type) graphic so be careful if you plan to resize it. If you increase its size too much then the image will become "blocky", with the pixels clearly visible

3 Repeat the process if you need to include a series of screenshots

4 Remember to save your document. The screenshots are stored internally within the Word document, so you don't need to worry about locating separate graphic files on your computer or online

6 Document views

Here, we'll look at five different ways of viewing your document, plus some additional visual features.

In Read Mode, Word reformats the entire document to make the best use of the available screen space. Material is organized into screens rather than pages, so a break between pages may not be in the same place as a break between screens.

Read Mode is ideal when working with a tablet or touch-enabled computer, as the left and right arrow icons are easy to operate with your finger. You can also use swipe left or swipe right gestures to move through the document.

In Read Mode you can type a number then press Enter to jump immediately to that page; e.g. 6 + Enter to move to page 6.

Read Mode

Use Word's Read Mode if you're viewing, rather than writing or editing, a document.

Activating Read Mode

1 Make sure the Read Mode icon (shaped like a book) in the Status bar is selected

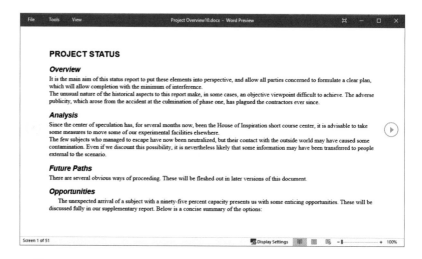

2 Use the left and right arrow icons, or the scroll bar at the bottom, to move between screens. The Status bar shows you the number of the current page

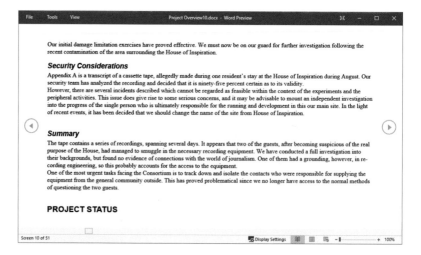

3 There is a Reading toolbar in the top-right corner. As well as the usual minimize, maximize and restore controls, you can also click 🔲 to auto-hide the toolbar and menus

Auto-hide Reading Toolbar

4 From the View menu you can show or hide the Navigation and Comments areas, and choose Page Color and Layout options

Hot tip

Click the 🔲 icon a second time to restore the toolbar and see the top-left corner menus again. You can also use the ⋯ icon to temporarily show the toolbar and menus.

5 Pictures will display at normal size for the document. However double-clicking with the mouse, or a double tap on a touchscreen will temporarily enlarge an image. Tap or click elsewhere to return to normal

Hot tip

If you click on the magnify icon, the picture will expand to maximum size. Then you can either click the icon a second time to reduce the image, or elsewhere on the screen to go back to reading your document.

...cont'd

Provided you haven't hidden the Reading toolbar, there are abbreviated menus in the top-left corner of the screen: File, Tools and View. If you open the Tools menu you can use the Find feature to locate text within the document.

6 If you close and then later reopen your document, Word remembers the location, so that you can carry on reading from where you left off. To do this, click on the message that automatically appears

Welcome back!
Pick up where you left off:

Summary 3
A few seconds ago

7 If you select and then right-click (or hold down your finger on a touchscreen) you'll see a pop-up menu of useful options including Smart Lookup and language translation. You can also add comments or highlights

Smart Lookup allows you to view a word's definition, listen to its pronunciation, and also to explore web resources such as Wikipedia and Bing.

8 You can use the zoom slider in the bottom-right corner to scale the text anywhere from 100% to 300% in size

If you have a touchscreen, you can zoom using the standard pinch and stretch gestures. This is very useful, particularly if you've hidden the Status bar with its zoom slider.

Accessing the other views

As you've seen already, you can use the View icons in the Status bar to switch views. However, this only gives you access to the three main views: Read Mode, Print Layout and Web Layout. There are two other views: Outline and Draft. To access any of the five views you need to go to the View tab.

Print Layout view

1 Go to the View tab and select Print Layout from the Views area, or click on the Print Layout icon in the Status bar

Hot tip

If you're currently in Read Mode first you'll need to switch back to either Print Layout or Web Layout view before you'll be able to access the View tab. Once there you can choose Outline, Draft or any of the other views.

2 This is the best view for general work as it gives you the full range of editing controls, together with a very accurate preview of how everything will look when printed. Scroll through your document and make some changes

3 Temporarily switch to Read Mode to see how both the display and the available controls change

4 When you save your document, Word will make a note of which of the main views (Read Mode, Print Layout or Web Layout) you used most recently, and switch to it the next time you open the file

...cont'd

Web Layout view

Web Layout view gives you a good idea of how your document would look if saved as a web page and then viewed in a browser such as Microsoft Edge.

1 Go to the View tab and select Web Layout from the Views area, or click on the Web Layout icon in the Status bar

Web pages often make use of hyperlinks for navigation, both within an article and to other articles and websites. See page 76 for more on creating hyperlinks.

134

2 To turn this into a web page, make sure you choose Web Page (*.htm, *.html) as the file type when saving

Although you've created a web page, for it to be available on the web it must be copied onto a server run by a web hosting service or Internet Service Provider. If you have an account with one of these then the company will be able to give you instructions on how to upload your files to their site.

Outline view

1 In the Views area of the View tab, click the Outline icon

Outline view is useful if you structure your document using headings and subheadings that are allocated to indented levels. The controls in the Outlining tab let you change levels, move lines up/down, or "collapse" items so that lines on lower levels are temporarily hidden from view.

Outline view is only suitable if your document uses at least two levels of heading and subheading – otherwise there is not enough structure for it to add any real value. Remember, Word's Print Layout view can also collapse and expand standard headings.

Draft View

1 In the views area of the View tab, click the Draft icon

The screen now shows a simplified view of your text, with elements such as graphics, headers and footers not visible.

2 This view is useful if your computer is slow, or if you just want to concentrate on the text with no distractions

3 You can continue to edit your text in this view. However, if you wish to see how your document will look when printed, return to Print Layout view by clicking the icon in the Views area of the View tab (or in the Status bar)

Gridlines

Defining and customizing gridlines

Gridlines are useful for helping you to align objects and resize them in a regular way.

Hot tip

Gridlines can be easily switched on and off from the Show controls in the View tab. To customize your grid, however, you need to follow the instructions on the right.

1 When you're working with a drawing object, the drawing tools appear automatically. Make sure the Format tab is active, click the Align icon in the Arrange area, and then choose Grid Settings

2 Here, you can set the size of the grid using "Grid settings". You can also control how many visible vertical and horizontal lines will be displayed. For example, if you set "Vertical every" to 2 then a visible line will appear for every second actual gridline. This is useful if you don't want your page cluttered with too many gridlines

3 Select "Display gridlines on screen" and then click OK

Don't forget

Gridlines do not print – they are there just to help you arrange items on the page. When the grid is active, objects will "snap" to the nearest gridline as if it were magnetic.

The Navigation pane

The Navigation pane can use the headings in your document to create a structured list located to the left of the main page area. This can be used to navigate easily through a long document.

Activating the Navigation pane

1 In the Show area of the View tab, click the Navigation Pane checkbox to switch it on

2 The Navigation pane appears, with its own scroll bars. It has three tabbed pages: Headings, Pages and Results. The first will list any headings or subheadings. If you click on one of these then the main document window will automatically move to this line, scrolling if necessary

3 The second tabbed page – Pages – will display the pages in your document as thumbnails (small images) so you can scroll visually through the document

4 The third tabbed page – Results – allows searching based on text or objects such as pictures, tables, or equations

5 When you're finished with the Navigation pane, either click the close icon in its top-right corner or switch off the option in the Show area of the View tab

A quick way to summon the Navigation pane with the Results tab active is to type Ctrl + F, as this is the shortcut for Find.

...cont'd

The Navigation pane can be used in a variety of ways. Here, we'll see some advanced examples using a document that has been structured with several levels of headings.

Browsing headings

1 Make sure the Navigation pane is visible. If not, select the View tab and click on the checkbox labeled Navigation Pane

2 Make sure the first of the three icons is selected at the top of the pane. This lists just the headings in your document

3 The network of headings and subheadings is displayed as a tree structure. If you click on the small triangle in this area, the sub-structure beneath this line will be collapsed (hidden) and revealed in turn

4 You can drag headings up and down to a different location, effectively restructuring your document very easily

5 Right-click on a heading to see options for adding, deleting, promoting, demoting, selecting, and printing headings

...cont'd

Browsing pages

1 Make the Navigation pane visible then click the second icon labeled Pages near its top. This allows you to browse by scrolling through small thumbnail images of each page

2 You can resize the Navigation pane by dragging horizontally on the vertical border between it and the main page. Also, you can drag on its title bar to make it a free-floating window

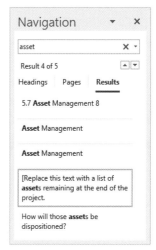

3 If you click on any thumbnail, the main window will scroll to the corresponding page

Browsing search results

1 If you click the small triangle beside the magnifying glass at the top of the pane you can browse through objects such as graphics, tables, or equations, as well as text

Hot tip

If the Results tab is active, and you're searching for text, you can see your results in context. Click on one of these and the main page will scroll to the appropriate location.

The Document Inspector

Before distributing your document to others, it's a good idea to check its content carefully. Sometimes your document might contain hidden information, or details you'd rather not include. The Document Inspector can help you with this.

1 Click on the File tab

2 The Info screen should appear by default (if not, then click on Info). Click on the "Check for Issues" button then select Inspect Document from the pop-up

The Document Inspector dialog lists different categories of content worth checking, some of which may be hidden but would be readable to someone with good technical knowledge.

3 Click the Inspect button. The results window appears

4 If you have any found items, you can get rid of them by clicking on the Remove All button. Click on Reinspect to verify the current state of play, then Close when done

7 Files and settings

In this chapter we'll see that the File tab looks very different to the others. It lets you take a step back and consider work at the file level as opposed to the contents of a document.

Info

1 With a document open, click on the File tab

2 By default, you'll see the Info screen. This gives you a useful summary of your current document's properties – listed along the right-hand side

3 In the central part of the screen there are controls for changing the permissions, checking for issues before sharing or distributing, and clearing up any draft versions of your document that may have been created automatically

4 If your current document is in a format for an older version of Word, you'll be missing out on some of the new features. If you want to upgrade it to the latest format, click the Convert button

Beware

If you do convert your document to the current Word format, others using earlier versions prior to Word 2010 may not be able to open it. If you need them to work on your document then use Save As and select "Word 97-2003 Document" as the file type (see next page).

Save to local file

1 Choose Save As, then select This PC to see this screen

You have the option to save to the Cloud, using a service such as OneDrive. This means you'll be able to access documents wherever there's an internet connection. See Chapter 8 for more details on sharing features.

2 To select a location, choose the current folder, one of the recently-used folders, or click the Browse button

3 Open the "Save as type" pop-up to see a list of file types. Useful types are PDF, Web Page, Plain and Rich Text

Plain Text is the simplest type – there's no formatting but your file will be readable on virtually any system.

4 Click on Tools and choose Save Options to control default settings such as file format and locations

5 Click OK and then Save to save your document

Recently-used files

1 Exit Word (if it's running) then start it up again

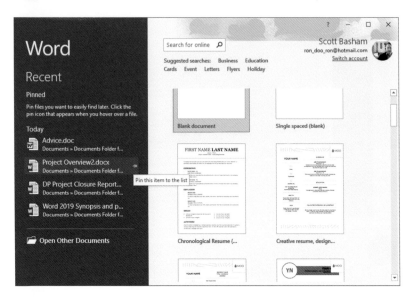

2 The left side of the screen will list your recently-used documents, so in most cases you'll just click one of these to resume work

3 If you hover over one of these a small pin icon ◼ appears. If you click this then the document will be "pinned"; i.e. permanently added to the list

4 The item will move to the top of the list, above a horizontal line, and the icon beside it will have changed to a vertical pin: ◼. Click this to "unpin" the item

5 If the document you want to open is not in the Recent list then choose Open Other Documents at the bottom of the screen

Hot tip

After the items you have pinned, the display of recent files is in order of modification date with the most recently modified first.

144

Opening local files

If Word is already running you can still use the File tab to open documents, although the screen design is slightly different.

1 Go to the File tab and choose Open

Recent files can include both online and locally-saved documents. For more on online shared documents, see Chapter 8.

2 There are five main options for locating your file. By default, Recent is selected. On the right-hand side you'll see the same list as in the previous example, with any pinned items at the top

3 If the document you want isn't there then click on This PC

4 You'll now see a list of folders, so select one of these to navigate manually to your file's location. Alternatively, from the Open screen choose Browse to access standard Windows browse-and-search facilities

The list of recent folders also has a pin/unpin facility, so you can make sure that your favorite locations are always easily accessible.

Opening other file formats

Word can open a range of file types, including .doc (the native type for older versions of Word) and .rtf (rich text format). Rich Text is a cross-platform standard for text, and has a reasonably extensive set of formatting features.

1 Click on the File tab and choose Open

2 Here, we opened an old document that was stored in the .doc format as read-only. If you look in the title bar you'll see both Read Only and Compatibility Mode noted in angle brackets

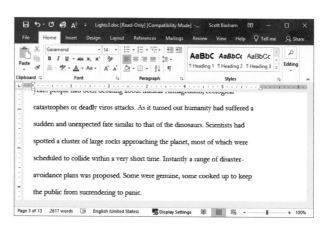

3 Go to the File tab and examine the Info screen

Note the indication that this is a read-only document. Also, Word's Compatibility Mode restricts available features to those from earlier versions of Word, so you can save and send to someone using the older software version.

4 Click Save As to create an editable copy. The .doc file type is used by default, but you can change this easily

Opening PDF files

Adobe Systems' Portable Document Format (PDF) is a very popular file standard for read-only documentation. A useful Word feature is the ability to open these and convert them into an editable format. You can then save in Word's own format, or re-export to PDF.

1 Click on the File tab and choose Open

2 Using any of the techniques covered in the previous examples, locate a PDF document

In this example, we've clicked on the Open dialog's View button and chosen "Large icons". This is useful as some files, such the PDF shown here, can show up with a small preview of their contents.

3 When you click Open, the following message will appear, reminding you of some of the limitations of PDF file conversion

4 Click OK. A progress bar will appear at the bottom of the main window while Word is performing the conversion

5 If the conversion is successful, the document will display in Print Layout view

PDF conversion is not always successful. For longer or more complex PDF documents, Word may run into difficulties and display an error message at this point.

LinkedIn

LinkedIn (owned by Microsoft) is a popular business social network designed to help people connect and share information related to their jobs, experience and skills. Microsoft Office applications are starting to provide integration with LinkedIn.

Integration with LinkedIn is a feature new to Word 2019 and Office 365.

1 Click on the File tab and choose Options. Scroll down within the General section to see LinkedIn Features

You can review your current login from the File tab, and also change this if necessary. For more details on online accounts, see page 156.

2 If you have a LinkedIn account based on your current login then click on "Manage LinkedIn account associations". This will take you to the LinkedIn website Account management page. If you have an appropriate account and Office installation then you'll have access to a Resume Assistant icon in Word's Review tab

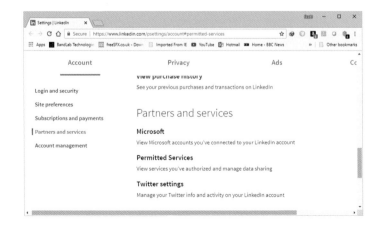

LinkedIn functionality can vary depending on whether you are using Word 2019 or Office 365. Microsoft's LinkedIn integration development is ongoing, so in Office 365 you may see changes in what is available from month to month.

Printing

1 Make sure you have an open document. Choose Print from the File tab

Hot tip

If you're printing on special paper then it's always worth clicking on the Printer Properties link. This will display the settings dialog for your particular make and model of printer, and will almost certainly contain controls for specifying paper type.

2 You'll see a preview of the current page, which is useful for checking margins and text flow. Click on the Forward and Back arrows at the bottom to move through the pages

3 Make sure the correct printer is selected, and that it is online. If your printer isn't listed, choose Add Printer

4 Review the other settings listed. If you don't want to print all pages then there are a number of other options available. For example, you could set a discontinuous range using "1-3, 5" (pages 1 to 3, followed by 5)

5 You can click on the Printer Properties link, or Page Setup, to access more detailed dialogs

6 Finally, go back to the top of the dialog, check the number of desired copies and then click Print

Using templates

Word has access to a wide range of templates, and has a useful screen for locating the right one for your needs.

 Click on New. In this screen you'll initially see a selection of the most commonly-used templates

Don't forget

To start off working with a single blank page, simply click the "Blank document" icon.

Hot tip

The Category pane on the right-hand side provides a way of narrowing down the results. Click on a category to see only the templates that are tagged with its name.

Click one of the suggested searches or enter your own search text. The example below searches for "agenda"

Scroll through the results and select a template

4 If you right-click on a template, a small pop-up menu appears. Choose Preview to learn more about the selected template

Hot tip

When previewing in this way you can use the left or right arrow icons to go to the previous or next template in the list.

5 If you're happy with your choice, click the Create button, or click on the background to return to the main screen

6 Once you open a template, you can edit and add to the sample text, then save the document under a new name

Hot tip

Although you're free to change settings such as font, size, spacing and color, it's usually best to stay with what was provided by the template. Most templates have their own particular design in order to allow you to concentrate just on the content.

...cont'd

Creating your own templates

A template is just an ordinary Word document saved as a special file type, and usually in a special location.

1 Create your document in the normal way. It may be worth using dummy placeholder text. When it's ready, choose Save As from the File tab and select a location

Tags make it easy for you to search for your templates later on. In this example, the company name "Virtual Resources" is being added as a tag, so that any searches using those words will return this template (plus any others with similar tags).

152

2 In the dialog, for "Save as type" choose Word Template (*.dotx). It's also good to set a title, and add some tags

3 Note that Word will, by default, save the file in a special Custom Office Templates directory (it's best not to change this if you want to be able to access your template easily in future). Click Save

4 Go to the File tab and choose Close. Then go back to the File tab and this time choose New, and click on the Personal heading to find your new template

In this example, make sure you click the word "PERSONAL" in capitals next to "FEATURED", and not the word "Personal" if listed under "Suggested searches". The latter would search for the word "Personal" in the template tags.

Options

We've already seen how to change certain options when we customized the Ribbon in Chapter 1. All these options and many more are available in one place via the File tab.

1 Make sure the File tab is active then click Options. The dialog that opens is organized into 11 sections, with General options displayed first

2 Unless your computer is very slow, keep On the options "Show Mini Toolbar on selection" and "Enable Live Preview". The latter controls what happens when you hover over a formatting feature; e.g. hovering over a style in the Style Gallery will temporarily show selected text in that format. "Update document content while dragging" enables the live preview when dragging objects

3 Click on the Trust Center section, then Trust Center Settings. This gives an overview of security and privacy settings, and also links to Microsoft policies and guidance

If you get an error message when attempting to open documents that were sent via email attachments, or were downloaded from the web, then first check you're sure they came from a reputable source. If you are, then go to the Trust Center Settings, click on the Protected View section, then clear the three checkboxes shown in the illustration on the left.

...cont'd

Many of the settings in the Word Options dialog have a small letter "i" in a circle next to them. If you hover over this you'll see a pop-up explaining what the setting does.

4 Click on the Display section to control whether Word displays non-printing characters such as tabs and paragraph marks

5 This dialog also has printing options so you can, for example, elect to print without drawings created in Word. This will speed up printing and save on printer ink – simple blank boxes will be printed in place of the graphics

6 Have a look at the other sections. The largest of these is Advanced, which contains extra settings for editing, display, printing, and saving

8 Sharing features

In this chapter we'll see how Word 2019 adds support for document portability and group working.

Roaming documents

In recent years Microsoft has added the ability to view and edit documents directly on the web, even if Word isn't installed on your computer. This means you're able to work on your files from any device with internet access, provided you've saved your document to a shared repository such as a Microsoft SharePoint server or a OneDrive storage area.

Using a shared area from Word

1 First, it's a good idea to review the services associated with your online account. Go to the File tab and then click on Account

Don't forget

For sharing to work properly, Word needs to know who you are. Normally the active account will be taken automatically from your Windows login. If this cannot be done then the first time you use Word you will be prompted for your username and password.

2 Check the account name and login listed under User Information. If this isn't you then click Switch account and enter your details

3 Now, look to see what is listed under Connected Services. Word may have already connected you to your OneDrive or Office 365 SharePoint service if linked to your login. It's also possible to connect to multiple shared storage areas – this is very useful if you plan to work with a group of people on the same documents

...cont'd

4 If you want to make use of a new Connected Service, then provided you have an appropriate active account, you can add one in. Click the "Add a service" button

5 Once you have set a Connected Service for storage it will show up in the Accounts section. You will be able to select it next time you save a document

Hot tip

Anyone with a Hotmail or Outlook web account will have access to a OneDrive area for shared document storage. Log in to **Outlook.com** to see this for yourself. If you do not have an account then it's free to set one up, or for an annual subscription fee you can sign up to an enhanced service with more storage space.

6 In this example, the current account has its own OneDrive connected service, and also access to another. Your account may be different to the above, so look for the cloud icon, which indicates an online shared area available to you. If you click on this, then the right-hand side of the dialog will display folders you have accessed recently. Click to specify where your file will be saved

...cont'd

 7 You will now see the directory structure of your online storage area. Double-click to move into a sub-directory

This is still the standard Windows Save As dialog, so you have access to the normal features for searching, navigating and displaying files, as well as viewing icons with preview if available. The file path shown at the top will depend on how your Connected Service is set up – in some cases it will be a local directory on your hard disk, which your system will automatically keep in sync with the online equivalent.

8 When you've found the right location, enter your file name and click Save

Don't be tempted to change file type at this stage, unless you have a specific reason for doing so. Word's web-editing features will require you to use the standard native file format.

9 Now, you can close your document, or carry on editing. If you edit it and then click Save, the online location will be updated just the same as for a local file on your hard disk. As long as your computer is always online, you can use the Cloud storage as your main repository for documents and, as we shall see, this has quite a few advantages

...cont'd

Accessing documents from Word Online

Imagine you're away from your main PC or tablet, and do not have access to an installed Microsoft Word. Word Online gives you the ability to read and edit documents directly within a web browser. In the following example, we'll access the Word document that was stored in OneDrive on the previous page.

1 Use a web browser to log in to your **Outlook.com** account

2 At the top left of the screen, click on the icon to the left of the Outlook title to see the following 15 application tiles

You can also invoke Word Online from **Outlook.com** via OneDrive. Click on OneDrive and navigate to your saved file, then right-click and choose Open in Word Online.

3 Click on the Word tile to see the screen below. Choose a document to edit from the Recent list, or click "Open from OneDrive" to browse for a file

159

...cont'd

4 The document opens in edit mode. You can see its name and location in the blue title bar at the top

If you're using a device with Word installed, you might prefer to choose the "Edit in Word" option. In this illustration it's in the top-right area just above the Styles section of the tool palette.

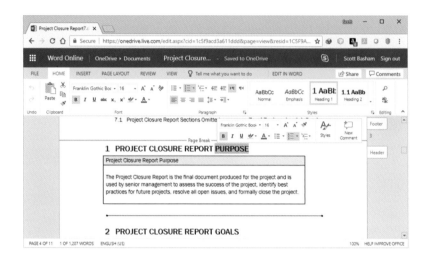

5 You'll see a web version of the familiar Word screen. Although there are fewer controls compared with the desktop version, it's still a very useful range of features

6 Experiment by reformatting some text or graphics. In this example we have changed the appearance of a table

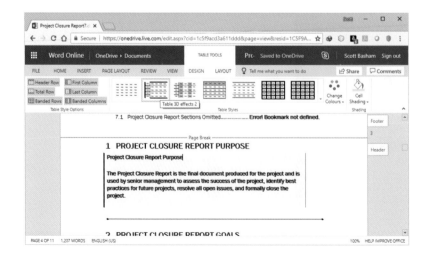

7 Click on the File tab, choose Info and have a look at the options. The "Edit in Word" button will invoke the normal desktop version of Word if available

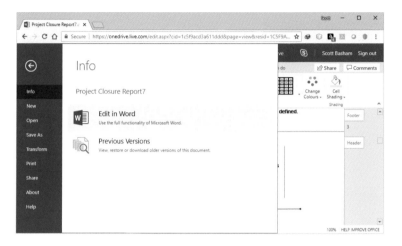

Note that the File tab contains Save As but there isn't a simple Save. This is because saving of the current file is handled automatically by Word Online.

8 Click on the left arrow icon to return to editing view. In the blue bar near the top you'll see the file location, its name, and a message that is normally "Saved to OneDrive"

9 Make an edit and you'll see the message change briefly to "Saving" (while Word Online updates the file stored in OneDrive), as in the example below

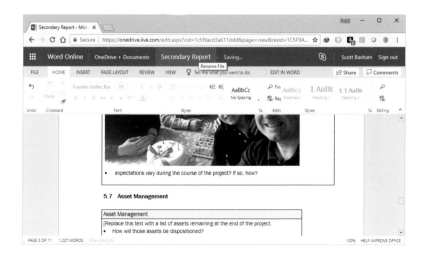

You can easily rename the current document. Simply click in the central blue area near the top where the document name is displayed and then edit or retype.

Working together

Once you have a document in a shared area such as OneDrive, you can collaborate with a number of co-authors. It's even possible for multiple users to work on the same document simultaneously; the key restriction being that only one person can edit a particular item at any time.

Preparing to share

1 In this example, we'll take a locally-stored document and go through the process of setting it up for online collaboration. Go to the File tab and choose Share

2 First, we must save to a shared location, so click the "Save to Cloud" button

3 The standard Save As screen appears. Choose your online location from its main icon and then select a folder

4 Enter the file name and click Save

5 Go back to the File tab and choose Share again. You'll see a "Share with People" option available. Click on this

Hot tip

Once you've started sharing you can use the Share pane to invite more people to share the document at any time, rather than going via the File tab.

6 In the new Share pane, enter the name or email address of another person who will access the document

7 Choose either "Can edit" or "Can view" for this person and, optionally, add in a message. There is also a "Get a sharing link" option that can generate a hyperlink for pasting into an email

...cont'd

8 Once you've clicked the Share button you can go ahead and add in more people as required. Anyone you add in will be contacted online

9 The person(s) you nominated will receive an email similar to the example below. Clicking on the "View in OneDrive" button will allow viewing and, if allowed, editing of the shared document. It isn't necessary for those you nominated to have Word installed, as the online version can be used for viewing and editing

Multiple users working on one document

In the previous example, Michael received an email advising him that he could work on our file. The email contained a hyperlink that would take him straight to that document. There, he would have the choice of using Word Online or the full version of Word (depending on what's available to him) to start editing. In this example, we'll start editing the document at exactly the same time as both Michael and a third user as well.

1 Go to the File tab and make sure the Info area is active

Here, you can see here the people currently working on your document

In the illustration underneath Step 2, the Share pane is visible to the right of the main document window. If you do not see this then click the blue Share button at the very top right of the screen.

2 Return to the document and keep a look out for any sign of Michael's and Steve's activities. In the example below, color-coded indicators appear, showing you where each person is editing. Word often operates a paragraph-level locking mechanism, so if someone else is editing a paragraph you can view but not change it

Make sure the setting "Automatically share changes" is set to "Always" (as in this example) to allow everyone to see edits in real time.

...cont'd

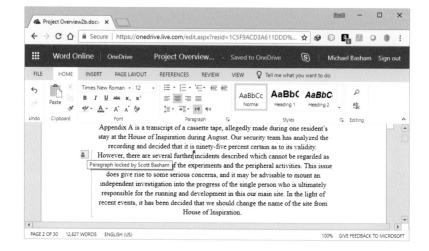

Hot tip

It is not always necessary for Word to lock the entire paragraph. If it assesses that it's safe to do so, it will let more than one person make changes. In this example, however, we can see that Word has decided to give Scott a lock over the whole paragraph until he completes his current edits.

3 In this example, Michael is the current user. You can see an indicator in the left margin indicating that Scott is working on the first paragraph. If Michael makes an attempt to edit within that paragraph Word will not allow this until Scott has completed his task

4 We can invoke a communication pop-up by right-clicking on any of the names in the Share pane. In this example, Michael is configured for email only, so we can send a message by clicking on the small envelope icon

Click here to send an email to the designated user

Adding people to the shared session

1 From the Word Online editing session, click the blue and white Share button in the top right corner

2 Enter the email address and a message. If you click on "Recipients can edit", you can choose to give either edit or view-only permissions

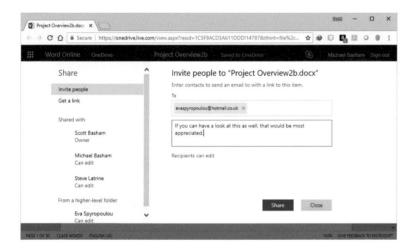

Removing people from the shared session

1 If you are the owner of the session, you can right-click on a name in the Share pane and choose Remove User

Hot tip

As you can see in this example, the session owner can also right-click and change the user's permission between "Can edit" and "Can view".

...cont'd

Skype

If the people collaborating on the document have Skype accounts, then it's very easy to start a Skype conversation while all the editing takes place.

Hot tip

A Skype conversation with multiple people initially has the same name as that of the Word document. To rename the conversation, click the pencil icon lower down in the panel.

1 In Word Online there is a Skype icon next to the Share button near the top of the window. Click on this to invoke the Skype functionality

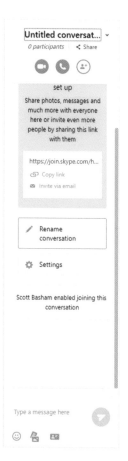

2 A Skype conversation panel is created. You can now find people to invite to the conversation using the search facility near the top of the panel

3 The icons at the top of the panel can be used to start video or audio, or to select new participants using Skype contacts. You can also enter a text message in the area at the bottom

Document updates

Managing changes manually

If you find constant real-time edits by multiple authors distracting, you can revert to a more manual process.

1 From the Share pane, set "Automatically share changes" to Never

2 Continue to edit your document. In this example, there is at least one other user editing this using Word Online

3 Go to the File tab. If other edits have been made then you will see the Document Updates Available message

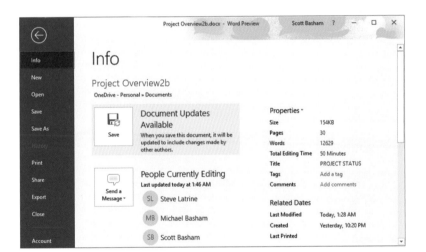

4 If you click Save then your document will be updated to correctly reflect all of the changes made by others. You may see the message below

Be very careful about allowing multiple authors to work simultaneously on a document, particularly if you are not automatically sharing changes in real time. It's a good idea to allocate separate and distinct roles. For example, one person could make the main edits while another proofreads. The proofreader would not edit the text, but instead add comments. See Chapter 10 for more on comments and reviewing.

Email

Many people like to attach Word documents and other types of file to email messages. If you have email client software such as Microsoft Outlook installed on your computer, you can send emails directly from Word.

Sending from Word

1 Once your document is ready for emailing, it's a good idea, first of all to Save it

Don't forget

If you do not have email client software, perhaps because you always use browser-based email, then your best option is to save your Word document locally. Then create a new message in your email browser page and use its feature for adding attachments.

2 Then, go to the File tab and click Share

3 Select Email and then choose the option "Send as Attachment"

Hot tip

If your document has been saved to a shared location then you will have an additional option: "Send a Link". This adds a hyperlink to your email. If the recipient clicks on this, he/she will be taken to the online file.

4 Provided your email client software is correctly installed, it will open with a new blank message. The Word document will automatically be added as an attachment

5 Note you can also send in other formats such as PDF

Present Online

With Word you can easily present your document to a group of
people via the web.

1 Open the document and scroll through to check what
you'll be presenting. In particular, check that each page is
a suitable shape and size for a screen presentation. Make
sure your document has been saved

This feature is also
available, more
appropriately, in
PowerPoint – the
application within the
Microsoft Office suite
specifically designed for
presentations.

2 When you're ready, go to the File tab and choose Share.
Click on the Present Online option on the left, and then
the button with the same name on the right-hand side

...cont'd

3 The document is sent to a Microsoft website, which acts as a free hosting service for the presentation. Once preparation is complete, you'll see a message similar to the one below

4 A URL (hyperlink) is generated. If you have a client email program such as Outlook installed, you can click on "Send in Email" to send this to your intended participant(s). Otherwise, copy and paste the link into an email message or instant messaging system

5 Once you have given your audience the URL, click Start Presentation. You can now see your document with a special Present Online tab of controls

Hot tip

If you have Microsoft OneNote installed, you can click on Share Meeting Notes to let your audience see notes you've prepared.

6 Anyone receiving your email or message can click on the URL to view the live presentation

7 As you move through your document, the people viewing the presentation will see their screens change too

8 During the presentation you can make changes to the document, if you first click the Edit button in the Present Online tab

Sometimes the receiving email client software doesn't support clicking on a URL for going automatically to a web page. If this is the case, then the URL can simply be copied to the Clipboard then pasted into the URL or Web Address area of the chosen browser.

173

9 You can send out additional invites by clicking the Send Invitations button. This shows the dialog we saw previously so you can access the URL and then send it to new invitees

10 When you have finished, click End Online Presentation to see the dialog below. You can either Cancel to resume presenting, or click End Online Presentation to close and return to Word's normal screen

Blogging

Blogs are websites that consist of a number of entries, or posts. These are usually arranged and presented in date order, with the most recent first. To publish your own Blog, you need to set up an account with a provider such as WordPress or Blogger. Often these are free to set up, although you can pay for a premium service with more storage and options to customize formatting.

Posting to a Blog

1 Create and edit a document in the normal way

Don't forget

Remember that your Blog Service will have its own style that will be applied to the text, so don't worry too much about formatting and design when creating your Word document.

2 When you're ready, go to the File tab and choose Share

3 Click "Post to Blog" to see the following dialog. Click the second button, also marked "Post to Blog", on the right-hand side of the screen

4 A new document will be created in Blog Post format, and your text copied in. Replace the text [Enter Post Title Here] with a suitable title

Hot tip

If you save this document it will retain its Blog Post property so you can use it as a starting point for re-posting. Also, when you manually create a new document, if you search the Templates list for "Blog" you'll be able to use the "Blog post" blank template. This will give you a pre-formatted document with the Blog Post tab already available.

5 If you haven't used Blogging before, click on the Manage Accounts button in the Blog tools then click New

6 In the New Blog Account dialog choose your Blog provider then click Next

Hot tip

You should have been given a username and password by your Blog Service Provider. If you're not sure what to enter for Blog Post URL then click the "Help me fill out this section" hyperlink for guidance appropriate for each provider.

7 Fill out your Blog Post URL, username and password (and select Remember Password if you'd prefer not to enter it every time you post) then click OK

...cont'd

8 Click Yes to the Warning dialog that appears. If your account details were correct you'll see the following confirmation message

9 A new entry will be listed in the Blog Accounts dialog, so posting to your blog will be very easy from now on. Click Close to return to the main document

10 Back in the main window, click the Publish tool in the Blog Post tab. A message will appear near the top confirming the date and time of the post

11 Repeat this process whenever you need to re-post

Don't forget

Now is a good time to go to your Blog website and have a look at the new post. If you need to change anything, you can edit in Word then click Publish again. Alternatively, most Blog Service Providers will allow you to edit posts via their own site.

9 References and mailings

In this chapter we'll look at more formal documents, covering indexing, Tables of Contents, and other types of references. We'll also look at creating automatic sequences of standardized documents.

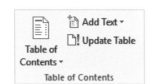

Table of Contents

You can automatically create a Table of Contents by asking Word to look for instances of particular styles, or by using entries that you create manually.

Creating a Table of Contents

1 Open a suitably long document that uses a structure of style headings. Make sure the References tab is active so you can see the Table of Contents controls on the left

2 Click the "Table of Contents" button and choose one of the available preset styles

3 Word looks through your document and uses the headings to generate the Table of Contents. It calculates the correct page number reference and adds it to each entry

4 Note that the entries generated in the Table of Contents reflect the heading structure in the main document. They also behave like hyperlinks: Ctrl + Click on any of these to jump straight to the relevant page

Hot tip

If you're using Web view then the Table of Contents entries will be displayed with actual hyperlinks rather than page numbers, as you can see below.

Manually adding or removing items

1 Select some text that is not already in the Table of Contents, then click the Add Text button and choose a Level number. The next time the Table of Contents is created or fully updated, the new entry will appear

...cont'd

2 To remove an item, select some text that is already in the Table of Contents, then click the Add Text button and select "Do Not Show in Table of Contents"

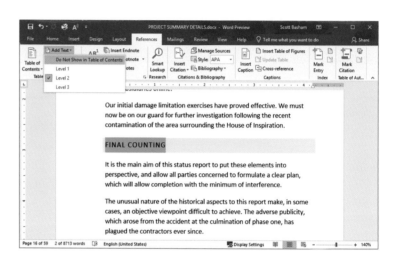

You can check at any time whether a piece of text is currently included in the Table of Contents. To do this, select the text then click the Add Text tool to see if it's currently assigned to any particular level.

Customizing your Table of Contents

1 Select a line in the Table of Contents and use the Styles Inspector to view its style

2 If you redefine this style then Word will automatically change all the entries of the same type. The new formatting will apply even if you recreate the table later

...cont'd

Updating your Table of Contents

1 As you continue to work with your document, text may move to different pages, pages may be inserted or deleted, and new headings may be added

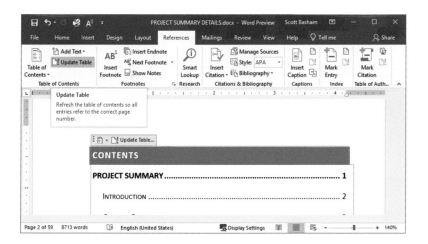

2 Click Update Table to rebuild the Table of Contents. You'll be given the choice of updating the entire table or just the page numbers of the existing entries

If you've added or removed items for your Table of Contents then make sure you select "Update entire table" rather than "Update page numbers only".

Manually defining your Table of Contents

When you click the "Table of Contents" tool to create the Table of Contents, as well as the predefined styles there's an option "Custom Table of Contents". In the dialog that appears, click Options to choose which text styles to use.

Footnotes and endnotes

These allow you to add a superscript number to a word or phrase that relates to explanatory text at the bottom of the page (for footnotes), or the end of the document or section (for endnotes).

Adding a footnote

1 Select the desired text and click Insert Footnote or press Ctrl + Alt + F

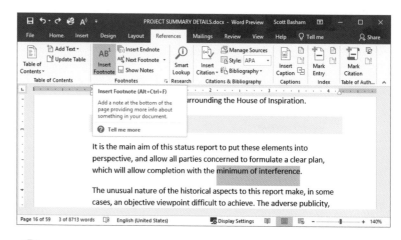

2 Next, add the footnote text at the bottom of the page

3 Note that the text you'd highlighted now includes a superscript footnote number. If you hover over this text, the footnote will temporarily appear as a pop-up

Don't forget

If you add new footnotes earlier on in your document, Word will automatically renumber the rest so that numbering is continuous.

Adding an endnote

1 Select the text and click Insert Endnote

Hot tip

The keyboard shortcut for inserting an endnote is Ctrl + Alt + D.

2 Enter the text for your endnote in the space provided

Hot tip

When you insert a footnote or endnote, the display automatically scrolls to the footnote or endnote area, ready for you to type in the text.

3 The Show Notes button will take you from the footnote back to the related text in the main part of the document

4 If you click the button a second time, you'll be taken to either the footnote or the endnote area

...cont'd

Navigating through footnotes and endnotes

1 Click the Next Footnote icon to see its pop-up menu

2 There are four options, allowing you to jump straight to the next or to the previous footnote or endnote

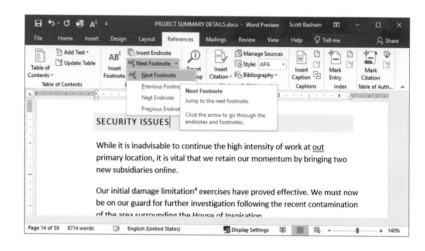

The Footnote and Endnote dialog

1 Click the icon in the lower right corner of the Footnotes area to see the Footnote and Endnote dialog

Here, you can specify where the notes are positioned – endnotes can go either at the end of the document or just at the end of the current section.

The number format defaults to Roman numerals for endnotes, but there are other options available.

You can also have different dialog settings for each section if you require that level of control.

Citations

Citations are useful if you need to add a reference to another author or publication within your text. Later on you can compile a standard bibliography that collects together all your citations.

Adding a citation

1 Click just after the reference in your main text. Click the Insert Citation button and choose Add New Source

2 The Create Source dialog appears. Choose the source then enter the details and click OK

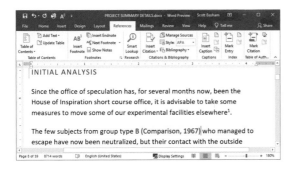

3 A short citation reference now appears next to your text. If you need to change any of the details you entered then click the Manage Sources button

Don't select the text, or the Insert Citation button will replace it with the citation. Instead, make sure you click after the main text, where you'd like the citation inserted.

If you've already added sources to your document, then you can select one of these from the pop-up menu attached to the Insert Citation button. This allows you to refer to the same source several times without rekeying the details.

Captions

Insert Caption

Insert Table of Figures
Update Table
Cross-reference

Captions

You can also add captions to equations and tables – follow exactly the same procedure.

1 Select your element then click on the Insert Caption icon in the References tab

2 Add the caption text to the dialog. There are three label options – Equation, Figure and Table (you can also use the New Label button to add more options). Choose Figure for this example

3 Captions will normally be numbered 1, 2, 3, and so on, but this can be changed by clicking on Numbering. Repeat the process to add more captions (you don't need to add these in any particular order)

Tables of figures

Once you've created captions throughout your document, you can ask Word to build a Table of Figures.

1 Make sure your insertion point is placed where you want the Table of Figures

2 Click on Insert Table of Figures

The Table of Figures dialog appears as shown.

3 Choose a format from the pop-up list. The Print and Web Preview areas will show you how this will look. Click OK to generate the table

4 If you make changes to your document, you should probably refresh the table. To do this, right-click somewhere within the table and choose Update Field

As with footnotes seen on page 182, Word automatically renumbers captions as you add to or delete from your document.

Indexing

Longer documents benefit greatly from a well-organized index. Word makes the process of creating an index fairly easy.

1 Select the text you want to add to the index, and click on Mark Entry (in the References tab) or press Shift + Alt + X

2 You can now edit the entry text, add a subentry, and choose whether the index will show the current page, a range of pages, or a cross-reference to another index entry

3 Use the Bold and Italic checkboxes if you want your index entry to be emphasized

4 When you have finished making your settings, click Mark, or Mark All if you want to mark all instances

5 This dialog is *non-modal*, which means that you can continue to work on the main page with the dialog still open. In this way, you can go right through your document, quickly and easily marking new entries, without having to continually reopen the dialog

6 As soon as you mark an entry, Word switches on the Show/Hide ¶ feature so you can see your index entries marked clearly as "tags" with curly brackets

You can toggle the Show/Hide ¶ feature On and Off with Ctrl + *.

7 Place your insertion point where you'd like the index, then click Insert Index to see the finished result

You can display the Style Inspector with the following: type Alt + Ctrl + Shift + S to summon the Styles panel then click on the ⬚ icon at the bottom.

8 Click in one of the entries in the new index then use the Style Inspector to see how it is automatically formatted

9 Word uses special styles (Index Heading, Index 1, Index 2, and so on) to control the formatting. If you edit these styles, rather than the index text directly, then your formatting decisions will be preserved even if you rebuild the index later on

If you edit your document so that the page numbers have changed, or if you have added more index entries, then you will need to rebuild the index. To do this, select the index and then click on Update Index.

Envelopes and labels

Envelopes   Labels

Create

Creating envelopes

1 Activate the Mailings tab and, in the Create area, click Envelopes. The following dialog appears

2 Enter the delivery address and, optionally, the return address. Click the Options button to select the envelope's design and dimensions from a list of standard sizes

Hot tip

As well as the Envelope Options, this dialog has a tab for Printing Options. This lets you tailor the settings to match the way you load envelopes into your printer.

3 Click Add to Document

4 If you entered a return address, you'll be shown a dialog asking you whether you want to make this the default return address. If you click Yes, then you won't need to retype it the next time you create an envelope

5 Once you click OK in the dialog box, your envelope will be generated on a new page

Creating labels

1 Click the Labels tool. The following dialog box appears

2 Enter the text (usually an address) and choose between creating a single label or a full page of the same label

3 Click the Options button, select the label vendor and then the label from the product numbers listed

4 Click the Details button to review the attributes of the currently-selected label

5 If you can't find the right label then click Cancel to return to the Label Options dialog, then click on New Label

6 Click OK to return to the Envelopes and Labels dialog, then choose New Document to generate your labels

7 Your labels will be generated on a new page

Mail Merge

There are several ways of setting up mail merging in Word, but the easiest is to use the Wizard, which guides you through the various stages of the process.

Using the Mail Merge Wizard

1 Click Start Mail Merge (in the Mailings tab) and select "Step-by-Step Mail Merge Wizard"

2 The Mail Merge window appears at the right-hand side of the screen. If you drag on its title bar you can make it into a floating window. Select the document type then click Next to be guided through the steps

3 In Step 3 you'll be prompted to specify a list of addresses. This can be from a variety of data sources, such as your Outlook contacts, or can be entered manually

4 You can then write your document using special fields or placeholders, which are then substituted with values from each address before printing

Mail Merge can be a real time saver if you've a long list of recipients. However, if you've only one or two then it's probably easier to create your documents manually.

Fields within Word appear as a name surrounded by angle brackets; for example: <<AddressBlock>>. Although you do not yet see the text that will be substituted for this placeholder, you can still control its positioning and formatting using the normal editing controls.

10 Tools for reviewing

This chapter looks at various ways of checking your work. We'll see how to manage your own edits or even changes made in collaboration with others.

Proofing Tools

Word can access a number of English and non-English dictionaries, which it uses when running spelling or grammar checks.

Hot tip

Rather than the whole document, you can also check just a section of text by selecting it in the normal way before clicking the Spelling & Grammar button.

1 As you type, Word will automatically check your spelling using its default dictionary. Any suspect words will be underlined in red with a wavy line. Right-click on each word to see your choices

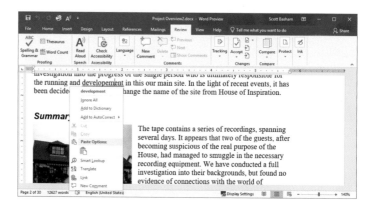

2 Click on one of the suggestions to make the correction

NEW

The new Proofing pane will also allow you to select one of the suggestions and then choose either Read Aloud or Spell Out from its attached menu. You will need to make sure you have an active sound card in your computer (with the volume unmuted) for this to work.

3 Click Ignore All if you'd like the highlighted word to be exempt from spell checking. Alternatively, click "Add to Dictionary" to add in the highlighted word

4 To run a check on your whole document, click the Spelling & Grammar button in the Proofing area of the Review tab. A Proofing pane will appear with all the necessary controls and information

5 Once you've made a decision to change, ignore or add to the dictionary, Word will resume its search for mistakes. If it finds a problem with grammar then the Proofing pane will switch from Spelling to show the Grammar controls, as in the example below

Another useful tool in the Review pane is the Accessibility Checker. Clicking on this will reveal a new pane that will inspect your document for issues which may limit how accessible is your document to people with varying needs, or people who work on devices with varying capabilities.

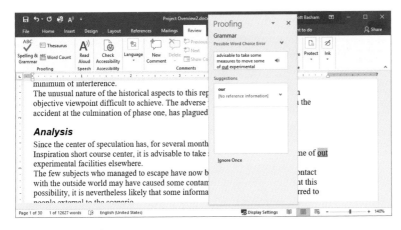

6 Review the suggestions and choose one if appropriate. You could also right-click on the word(s) in the document and choose Ignore, or simply manually edit the text

7 When Word has finished looking through the document, it will display a "check complete" message

The Read Aloud tool

Another useful tool in the Review pane is the Read Aloud tool. This will use synthesized speech to read out either your entire document or just the text you have selected.

When using the tool, the following appears:

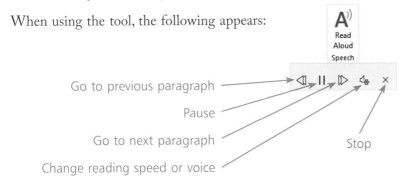

Go to previous paragraph

Pause

Go to next paragraph

Change reading speed or voice

Stop

The Read Aloud tool is a feature new to Word 2019, although earlier versions do have a more basic word-reading capability.

Smart Lookup

1 Select a word or phrase and right-click to see the pop-up menu

2 Choose Smart Lookup. The Smart Lookup panel will appear, showing you the results of web searches based not just on your text, but also the words that surround it. This helps you to find information that is relevant to the context of your document

Translating selected text

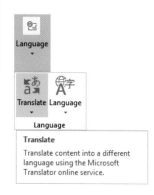

1 Select one or more words, then click on the Language tool in the Review tab. In the pop-up menu that appears, choose Translate Selection

2 In the special Translator pane that appears, make sure that English is selected in the From field, and the target language in the To field

3 The translated text appears in the lower half of the Translator pane. If you'd like to use the translated text, click on the Insert button

Translation has been improved with Word 2019 – the new tool makes the process easier, and is better integrated with the application.

Thesaurus

1 A Thesaurus is a collection of synonyms (words with identical or similar meanings). Select a word then click on the Thesaurus icon in the Proofing area of the Review tab

2 The Thesaurus pane appears – this can be moved or resized simply by dragging with the mouse. It contains a list of synonyms for the word you selected

3 Scroll though and select one of the options. The word will be moved to the main field at the top, and the list will now show you synonyms for that word

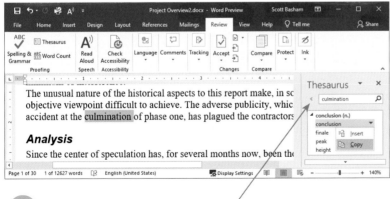

4 To go back one level, click the ◀ icon

5 If you right-click in the list, from the pop-up menu that appears you can choose to insert the selected item, or copy it to the Clipboard

Hot tip

A quicker way to access the Thesaurus is to select a word, right-click, then choose Synonyms from the pop-up menu.

Comments

Adding a comment

1 Select the text to which you'd like to add a comment

2 Make sure the Review tab is active, then click the New Comment icon in the Comments area

Comments are automatically logged with your username, and the time they were made. This is useful if several people are reviewing a document.

3 Add the comment text in the Markup area at the right

4 Repeat this process to add more comments

If you allow your mouse to rest over a commented piece of text, the comment will appear as a tooltip. This is useful if you cannot see the Markup area (if you are working in Draft mode, for example).

5 To delete a comment, click on it and then click the Delete icon

6 You can move through the comments in your document using the Previous and Next buttons

7 You can also delete all comments from the Delete pop-up

...cont'd

Multiple users adding comments

We saw in Chapter 8 that many users can access the same document, sometimes even at the same time, if the file is in a shared area. The Comments feature takes account of this.

1 In this example, Michael and Scott are logged in to Word Online and are writing comments in the document we saw on the previous page

In this illustration you can see that Word assigns different colors to different users for comments.

199

2 We can clearly see which comments are made by which person. Scott clicked on the Reply icon to respond to Michael's comment

3 This process can repeat, with the first user commenting on the second user's comment

Marking a comment as done

Once an exchange of comments has ended with a satisfactory conclusion, you can mark them as Resolved. This will change them to a light-gray color so that they are less distracting, although you can still see them in case you need to change your mind later on.

1 Select a comment to see the icons for Reply and Resolve

2 Choose Resolve to complete the interaction. You can also select a closed comment and choose Reopen. Right-click for further options including Delete Comment

Ink

Adding Ink to your document

If you have a suitable pen device, Word has an Inking feature that allows you to write by hand over the main page. Microsoft Office has Inking features across its range of applications, although its exact implementation does vary according to software version.

Some Word versions include the facility to add Ink Comments using a tool in the Comments area of the Review tab. As with ordinary comments, Word adds the username and timestamp to whatever is written.

1 Open a document in Print Layout view. Make sure the Review tab is active

2 Click the Start Inking tool and get your pen ready

3 Use the Pen tool to write anywhere on your document. This will create an overlay on top of the document contents, without changing them

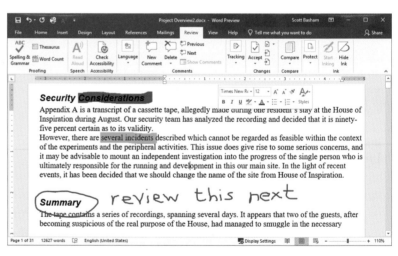

4 If the Start Inking tool is inactive then this may be because you do not have a suitable pen device available and configured

Tracking

Sometimes it's useful to track changes you make to a document, so that someone else can see exactly what you've done. It may even be necessary for someone to approve or reject those changes before they become permanently incorporated into the document.

1 To activate change tracking, click the Track Changes icon in the Tracking area of the Review tab

If you rest your mouse over any changed text, then the name, type of change, and date/time appears as a tooltip.

2 Now, your edits will be shown visually. Experiment by deleting text, adding in some new text, editing existing text or changing format

3 Use copy and paste to move a phrase, sentence or paragraph to a different part of your document

Deleted text can either be shown in a different color with a horizontal line running through it, or noted in the right margin. A vertical line in the margin indicates that changes were made in this area.

...cont'd

Hot tip

The Reviewing pane will list out all the tracked changes. Just below its title, there is a summary that shows you the total number of revisions. Clicking the ∨ icon beside it will toggle a breakdown summary of the types of revisions On and Off.

4 Click on the Reviewing Pane icon in the Tracking area, and choose one of the two options (Vertical or Horizontal) to make it visible

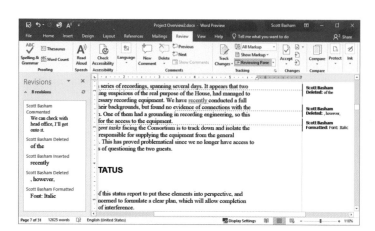

5 Make some more changes to your document and watch what happens in the Reviewing pane

6 The Reviewing pane contains a comprehensive summary of all the comments and revisions made. Clicking on an entry in the main list will take you to its location in the main document

7 Scroll through your document until you find a section with both comments and revisions (or make some new comments and revisions yourself)

8 Now, switch to Simple Markup so that you can appreciate the difference it makes. It's much easier to read – but you can still see comments by looking in the Comments area on the right-hand side

9 The Reviewing pane still shows you what's changed. Also, a vertical line to the left of the text indicates it has been altered. Click on this to see the tracked changes

Don't forget

10 You can also choose No Markup to see how the document would look when finalized, or Original to see how it was before any of the tracked changes

11 When collaborating with other authors via a shared document, Tracking is useful regardless of whether the users are editing simultaneously or at different times. The example below is a continuation from what we saw in Chapter 8. Here, you can see the color-coded activity of three users, all working together

Multiple panes can be active at any time. These illustrations show just the Revisions pane, but if the Navigation pane was also visible then these would normally be arranged next to each other on the left side of the screen. It's easy to switch panes on and off, or to move them to a different location.

...cont'd

Locking tracking

If you'd like to insist that tracking is switched on when you collaborate with others, then you can lock it On using a password.

1 Open the pop-up menu attached to the Track Changes icon in the Tracking area of the Review tab

2 Choose Lock Tracking

3 Enter a password, then once more to confirm, and click OK

Changes

Now, if there are changes in your document, you can take on the role of someone who reviews those changes. The tools in the Changes area let you work through your document looking at each change in turn – using the Previous and Next icons.

1 If you click the Accept button then the change is permanently applied to the document

2 If you click Reject, the change is removed and the text reverts to its original state

Protecting a document

Word allows you to protect your document in a number of ways. You can control which aspects may be edited: for example, you may allow a user to add comments but not to edit the text directly. If you are sharing your document you can also restrict permissions to certain users. Furthermore, you can set protection on the document as a whole.

Creating a document password

1 Make sure you have your document open. Go to the File tab – the Info section is displayed by default

2 Click Protect Document then "Encrypt with Password"

3 Enter a password, click OK, then enter it a second time to confirm

4 Save the document in the normal way. Make sure you remember the password you set

After you've set the password, the Info section in the File tab will remind you that a password is required to open the document.

...cont'd

Mark as Final

When you've finished editing your document you can "Mark as Final", indicating to anyone who opens it that this is the definitive version and should not be changed.

1 Go to the File tab and make sure the Info section is displayed

2 Click Protect Document and then "Mark as Final"

3 Save the document. The following message appears

Digital Signature

If you add a Digital Signature to a document, it can be used as a recognized form of authentication or approval that can be checked by others.

1 Go to the File tab and make sure the Info section is displayed. Click on Protect Document and choose "Add a Digital Signature". The following dialog appears:

2 Choose a Commitment Type then fill in the "Purpose for signing this document" field. Optionally, you can click "Details" to enter more information about yourself

Once a document is signed it is not expected to change, as this will invalidate the Digital Signature. Word will present the dialog below asking you to confirm that you want to go ahead – if you click Yes then any signatures are removed.

3 Click OK. The following message appears

4 On opening the document a user will see a message indicating there is a Digital Signature. Any attempt to edit the document will automatically remove the Signatures – if the document needs to change then it should be reviewed again and re-signed if appropriate

Opening a protected document

1 Go to the File tab and open the document you saved previously

2 A dialog appears prompting you for the password. Enter the password then click OK

3 If the document was marked as final then Word will automatically select Read Mode when it is opened. If there were any Inked annotations or comments, then at the top of the window you'll see two messages as shown in the following example

...cont'd

4 Go to Layout Mode and try to make some changes. You'll find you cannot change things, and instead there will be a "locked" message in the Status bar

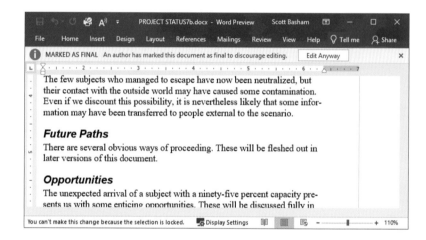

Restrict Editing

This offers better control over access to your document.

Restrict Editing

1 Click the Restrict Editing tool in the Protect area on the right-hand side of the Review tab. The Restrict Editing pane appears

2 Switch on "Limit formatting to a selection of styles" then click on Settings

3 From this dialog you can choose which styles are allowed. By default they're all enabled, so either review each one or, if you want to use just a few, click "None" then reselect the styles you wish to allow. Click OK when you've finished

Hot tip

If you switch on Editing restrictions and make sure the setting is "No changes (Read only)" then this prevents users from making any changes at all. This is more secure than the "Mark as Final" feature.

4 You may see the message below, asking you what you'd like to do with the styles you've forbidden

Microsoft Word ✕

? This document may contain formatting or styles that aren't allowed. Do you want to remove them?

Yes   No

5 Alternatively, you can limit users' activities in several other ways by choosing an option for Editing Restrictions. "Tracked changes" means that tracking is compulsory and cannot be switched off. Choose "No changes (Read only)" to fully protect your document

6 Make any last-minute changes to your document then, when you're ready, click "Yes, Start Enforcing Protection"

7 Enter a password, and then once again to confirm

8 Save and close the document

9 Now, reopen the document to check the level of protection

The Restrict Editing pane will remind you that the document is protected and you cannot make edits. If you change your mind you can click Stop Protection and enter the password to proceed.

Hot tip

If you're sharing your document online, you can manually lock the other authors out of certain areas. Select the text you'd like to reserve and then click the Block Authors icon in the Protect area of the Review tab. To release this area, reselect and click the icon a second time, then save the document.

Block Authors ▾

Add-ins

Add-ins enhance Word by giving you access to external services such as online dictionaries or research sources. They can also provide new interactive objects that enhance document content.

Reviewing available Add-ins

1 Go to the Insert tab and select "My Add-ins". You'll see the following dialog listing the Add-ins currently installed in Word

Hot tip

You can also click the "Get Add-ins" icon in the Add-ins area to go straight to the Store section of the Office Add-in dialog. Examples of Add-ins include utilities for adding QR codes to your document, sending faxes, and accessing Emojis.

2 Click on the blue hyperlink "Manage My Add-ins". You will be taken to Microsoft's Office Store where there is a special web page showing additional details such as licensing information, expiry (if appropriate), and the date the Add-in was first acquired

Hot tip

Open the pop-up menu for the "My Add-ins" control and choose "Manage Other Add-ins" to see technical information in Word's Options dialog.

3 Click on the "Add-ins" link at the top of the web page to browse for new items to add to Word or Office

Index